The Infortunate

Also by Susan E. Klepp:

The "Swift Progress of Population": A Documentary and Bibliographic Study of Philadelphia's Growth, 1642–1859

Philadelphia in Transition: A Demographic History of the City and Its Occupational Groups, 1720–1830

Also edited by Susan E. Klepp:

The Demographic History of the Philadelphia Region, 1600–1860

Also by Billy G. Smith:

The "Lower Sort": Philadelphia's Laboring People, 1750–1800

Also edited by Billy G. Smith:

Blacks Who Stole Themselves: Advertisements for Runaways in the Pennsylvania Gazette, 1728–1790

The INFORTUNATE

The Voyage and Adventures of WILLIAM MORALEY, *an Indentured Servant*

Edited with an Introduction and Notes by

SUSAN E. KLEPP

&

BILLY G. SMITH

The Pennsylvania State University Press

University Park, Pennsylvania

Library of Congress Cataloging-in-Publication Data

Moraley, William, 18th cent.
The Infortunate : the voyage and adventures of William Moraley, an indentured servant / edited with an introduction and notes by Susan E. Klepp and Billy G. Smith.

p. cm.
Originally published: Newcastle, 1743. With new introd.
Includes index.
ISBN 0-271-00828-8 (cloth)
ISBN 0-271-00844-X (paper)
1. Pennsylvania—Social life and customs—Colonial period, ca. 1600–1775. 2. Moraley, William, 18th cent. 3. Indentured servants—Pennsylvania—Biography. I. Klepp, Susan E. II. Smith, Billy Gordon. III. Title.
F152.M78 1992
917.4804'2—dc20 91-32324
CIP

Sixth printing, 2004

Published by The Pennsylvania State University Press
University Park, PA 16802-1003
Printed in the United States of America

It is the policy of The Pennsylvania State University Press to use acid-free paper for the first printing of all clothbound books. Publications on uncoated stock satisfy the minimum requirements of American National Standard for Information Sciences—Permanence of Paper for Printed Library Materials, ANSI Z39.48–1984.

For Jack Leon Smith, Edith Klepp Mueser, L. S. Klepp, and Maggie Klepp

CONTENTS

LIST OF ILLUSTRATIONS

Maps

Figures

EDITORS' PREFACE

Eighteenth-century America has been called the Age of Benjamin Franklin, an era best characterized by the values expressed in his autobiography and by his incredibly successful career. Yet Franklin was only one of several million inhabitants of the North American colonies, and by his own account he was both exceptionally hardworking and unusually fortunate.

But what if his luck had been different? What if Franklin's father had not acceded to his son's occupational choice, if the young runaway apprentice had been apprehended by authorities, if several well-established printers had dominated the trade in Philadelphia when Franklin arrived, if his creditors had sued to collect his debts, if his wife's first husband had returned and charged him with bigamy, if fornication charges had been brought at the birth of his illegitimate son, if illness or a large family had drained his resources, or if the local economy had stagnated at critical junctures in his career? Had any of these things happened, Franklin might well have been just another obscure artisan, invisible to all but the most persistent scholars.

During the last two decades, historians have expanded the scope of history by attempting to recover the experiences and contributions of the forgotten and less fortunate inhabitants of Britain and its American colonies. It is a difficult task, because so few artisans, laborers, sailors, slaves, and women left firsthand accounts of their lives. The editors of this volume have spent most of their academic careers analyzing tax lists, church registers, newspaper reports, probate records, and census schedules in an effort to recreate some of the daily physical experiences—including family, health, diet, income, housing, and work—of the middling and laboring residents of the eighteenth-century Mid-Atlantic region. But the thoughts, beliefs, hopes, and opinions of the majority remain elusive, even as our knowledge of their objective conditions has increased.

After toiling in the archives for years only to find scattered scraps of evidence, what a pleasure it was to discover the autobiography of William Moraley. Smart, sassy, and articulate, Moraley provides a considerably richer view of common experience in the eighteenth-century Anglo-American world than do most other sources. His memoirs depict the life of a down-and-out artisan whose fortune, like that of so many other immigrant bound workers, did not substantially improve. The autobiography also offers a complex perspective that can be read on numerous levels. In particular, it reflects the enigmas of the eighteenth-century Atlantic world in a series of unsettling juxtapositions: science and superstition, religion and roguery, industry and indulgence, fact and fiction, heroic ambition and humble subservience.

In many ways William Moraley lived out the worst-case scenario for eighteenth-century artisans. What succeeded for Franklin failed for Moraley. While Franklin marched from triumph to triumph, Moraley reeled from one misfortune to another. Was Moraley truly unfortunate or merely feckless? The reasons for the different career paths of men in the lower classes have been the subject of much scholarly debate. Moraley's memoirs can more firmly ground that controversy in actual human experience and contribute to our understanding of the eighteenth-century Atlantic world.

Just as history has often failed to credit those not in the limelight for their vital contributions to shaping the past and the present, so too do the conventions of authorship frequently obscure the cooperative and communal nature of historical research and writing. This preface allows a conventional, if less than fully adequate, opportunity to express our gratitude for the generosity, insight, and expertise of others.

Unlike Moraley, we have been very fortunate in pursuing this enterprise, and we wish to thank Farley Grubb, P. M. G. Harris, Bernard Herman, Craig Horle, Judy McGaw, Tom Slaughter, Marianne Wokeck, Michael Zuckerman, and members of the seminar of the Philadelphia Center for Early American Studies for their comments on the Introduction. The following people and institutions also kindly provided us with invaluable assistance: the Burlington County Historical Society and Rhett Pernot, Dorothy Eckert, and Kathy Heuer; Bert Denker and the staff at the Winterthur Museum and Library; Roy Goodman at the American Philosophical Society; Philip Lapsansky at the Library Company of Philadelphia; Dr. J. M. Fewster and Mrs. J. L. Drury of the Division of Archives and Special Collections of the University of Durham Library; Patricia Sheldon of the Newcastle Central Library and Constance M. Fraser of the Society of Antiquaries of Newcastle-upon-Tyne; and the staffs at the Genealogical Society of Pennsylvania, the Historical Society of Pennsylvania, Van Pelt Library at the University of Pennsylvania, Moore Library at Rider College, and the Family History Library of the Church of Jesus Christ of Latter-Day Saints in Broomall, Pennsylvania. The William Clements Library at the University of Michigan granted permission to print the complete edition of Moraley's autobiography which is part of their holdings. A Mellon Fellowship at the American Philosophical Society and research support from Montana State University helped the editors complete this book. Betty Smith and Richard Wojtowicz assisted in preparing the manuscript. And Peter Potter, the editor at Penn State Press, provided much needed encouragement and very helpful suggestions. We also gratefully acknowledge the support of our families throughout this project.

ABBREVIATIONS

AIS — Roland Vern Jackson, comp., *Early New Jersey, 1600–1819* (Bountiful, Utah: Accelerated Indexing Systems, 1981). Photo offset of computer-generated genealogical abstracts from the Family History Library of the Church of Jesus Christ of Latter-Day Saints.

GSP — Genealogical Society of Pennsylvania, housed at the Historical Society of Pennsylvania, Philadelphia.

IGI — International Genealogical Index, Church of Jesus Christ of Latter-Day Saints. Microfiche of computer-generated genealogical abstracts. Copies at the Family History Center, Pennsylvania Stake, Broomall, Pennsylvania. The origins and a description of this collection are available in Alex Shoumatoff, *A Mountain of Names* (New York: Simon & Schuster, 1985), esp. 227–93.

PMHB — *Pennsylvania Magazine of History and Biography.*

Wills — *New Jersey Archives*, First Series: *Documents Relating to the Colonial History of the State of New Jersey*, vols. 1–13, *Abstracts of Wills*, ed. A. Van Doren Honeyman (Somerville, N.J.: Unionist-Gazette, 1918).

EDITORS' INTRODUCTION

The writings of European visitors have served as invaluable sources for our knowledge about early America.[1] But wealthy travelers left most accounts, and they frequently saw the New World through the windows of fancy carriages and formed their opinions in conversations with the native elite. William Moraley's memoirs offer a decidedly different perspective.

William Moraley ventured from England to the colonies in 1729 as an indentured servant, worked in various capacities, rambled about the countryside on foot, and mingled with white and black bondspeople, laborers, artisans, Indians, and other common folk. While the very act of writing his memoirs makes Moraley unusual, his experiences were

1. Among the many journals left by travelers in the Mid-Atlantic region are Peter Kalm, *The America of 1750: Peter Kalm's Travels in North America*, ed. Adolph B. Benson, 2 vols. (New York: Dover Publications, 1964); J. P. Brissot de Warville, *New Travels in the United States of America, 1788*, ed. and trans. Durand Escheverria and Mara Soceanu (Cambridge, Mass.: Harvard University Press, 1964); and Kenneth Roberts and Anna M. Roberts, eds., *Moreau de St. Mery's American Journey* [1793–98] (Garden City, N.Y.: Doubleday, 1947).

similar to those of many eighteenth-century European migrants, the majority of whom sold themselves into servitude for three or four years in exchange for food, shelter, clothing, and passage to North America.[2] A large number of journals, diaries, and letters by wealthy early Americans survive, but autobiographies, wherein individuals reflect on the course and meaning of their lives, are rare. Benjamin Franklin's autobiography, written near the end of an exceptionally successful career, stands out as one of the few eighteenth-century American accounts.[3] More extraordinary still are memoirs of people like William Moraley who stood on the bottom rungs of American society and who, unlike

2. On eighteenth-century indentured servants, see the general studies of David W. Galenson, *White Servitude in Colonial America: An Economic Analysis* (Cambridge: Cambridge University Press, 1981); David W. Galenson, "Labor Market Behavior in Colonial America: Servitude, Slavery, and Free Labor," in David W. Galenson, ed., *Markets in History: Economic Studies of the Past* (Cambridge: Cambridge University Press, 1989), 52–96; Abbot Emerson Smith, *Colonists in Bondage: White Servitude and Convict Labor in America, 1607–1776* (Chapel Hill: University of North Carolina Press, 1947); Farley Grubb, "The Incidence of Servitude in Trans-Atlantic Migration, 1771–1804," *Explorations in Economic History* 22 (1985): 316–39; Farley Grubb, "The Market Structure of Shipping German Immigrants to Colonial America," *PMHB* 111 (1987): 27–48. Studies that focus primarily on servitude in Pennsylvania include Sharon V. Salinger, *"To Serve Well and Faithfully": Labor and Indentured Servants in Pennsylvania, 1682–1800* (Cambridge: Cambridge University Press, 1987); Cheesman A. Herrick, *White Servitude in Pennsylvania: Indentured and Redemption Labor in Colony and Commonwealth* (1926; reprint, New York: Negro Universities Press, 1969); Karl Geiser, *Redemptioners and Indentured Servants in the Colony and Commonwealth of Pennsylvania* (New Haven: Yale University Press, 1901); Farley Grubb, "Redemptioner Immigration to Pennsylvania: Evidence on Contract Choice and Profitability," *Journal of Economic History* 46 (1986): 407–18; Farley Grubb, "The Auction of Redemptioner Servants, Philadelphia, 1771–1804: An Economic Analysis," *Journal of Economic History* 48 (1988): 583–603; Farley Grubb, "The Market for Indentured Immigrants: Evidence on the Efficiency of Forward-Labor Contracting in Philadelphia, 1745–1773," *Journal of Economic History* 45 (1985): 855–68; Farley Grubb, "Servant Auction Records and Immigration into the Delaware Valley, 1745–1831: The Proportion of Females Among Immigrant Servants," *Proceedings of the American Philosophical Society* 133 (1989): 154–69; Frank R. Diffendorffer, "The German Immigration into Pennsylvania Through the Port of Philadelphia, and 'The Redemptioners,'" *Pennsylvania German Society* 10 (1899): 189–93; Marianne S. Wokeck, "German and Irish Immigration to Colonial Philadelphia," in Susan E. Klepp, ed., *The Demographic History of the Philadelphia Region, 1600–1860* (Philadelphia: American Philosophical Society, 1989), 128–43; Marianne S. Wokeck, "The Flow and the Composition of the German Immigration to Philadelphia, 1727–1775," *PMHB* 105 (1981): 249–78; and Marianne S. Wokeck, "Irish Immigration to the Delaware Valley before the American Revolution," in David B. Quinn, ed., *Ireland and America, 1500–1800*, forthcoming.

3. L. Jesse Lemisch, ed., *Benjamin Franklin: The Autobiography and Other Writings* (New York: New American Library, 1961); see also Frederick B. Tolles, ed., *The Journal of John Woolman* (New York: Corinth Books, 1961). A handful of blacks wrote memoirs, one of the most notable being *The Interesting Narrative of the Life of Olaudah Equiano; or, Gustavus Vassa, the African, Written by Himself*, ed. Paul Edwards, 2 vols. (London: Dawsons, 1969). See also Daniel B. Shea, *Spiritual Autobiography in Early America* (Princeton: Princeton University Press, 1968); and Angelo Costanzo, *Surprizing Narrative: Olaudah Equiano and the Beginnings of Black Autobiography* (New York: Greenwood Press, 1987).

Franklin, were unable to ascend the ladder. For all these reasons, Moraley's report provides a quite unusual perspective on life in America during the early decades of the eighteenth century.[4]

Moraley's travels in North America form the central event in his autobiography. Then, after spending nearly five years in the New World between 1729 and 1734, Moraley returned to England, where he wrote and published his *Voyage and Adventures* in 1743. As the title suggests, he designed his story both to inform and to entertain. After sketching a few incidents from his early life, he describes the persuasive agent who convinced him to sign an indenture as a bound servant and then the ocean voyage, his sale in Philadelphia, and his subsequent service as a "Voluntary Slave" (64).[5] Moraley's account brims over with observations on the middle colonies a half-century after their settlement by the English. He describes the geography and climate, the flora and fauna, and the customs, religions, superstitions, material conditions, and daily life of the inhabitants. Of particular interest are his comments about servants, slaves, and Native Americans—groups often ignored by early travelers. To enhance the entertainment value of his narrative, Moraley includes three short stories, examples of tales he might have told to pass the time on board ship or to regale his customers. Moraley's

4. Two accounts left by poorer eighteenth-century Americans are Israel R. Potter, *The Life and Remarkable Adventures of Israel R. Potter*, ed. Leonard Kriegel (1824; reprint, New York: Corinth Books, 1962); and Frank D. Prager, ed., *The Autobiography of John Fitch* (Philadelphia: American Philosophical Society, 1976). Autobiographies of indentured servants are especially rare, but see Daniel B. Shea, ed., "Some Account of the Fore Part of the Life of Elizabeth Ashbridge," in *Journeys in New Worlds: Early American Women's Narratives*, ed. William L. Andrews et al. (Madison: University of Wisconsin Press, 1990), 117–80; James Annesley, *Memoirs of an Unfortunate Young Nobleman, Returned from Thirteen Years' Slavery in America: A Story Founded on Truth and Addressed Equally to the Head and Heart* (London: Freeman, 1763); and Peter Williamson, *The Life and Curious Adventures of Peter Williamson, Who Was Carried Off from Aberdeen and Sold for a Slave* (Aberdeen: n.p., 1804). A few bound servants left letters and journals; see John Harrower, *The Journal of John Harrower, an Indentured Servant in the Colony of Virginia, 1773–1776*, ed. Edward Miles Riley (New York: Holt, Rinehart & Winston, 1963); Daniel Kent, *Letters and Other Papers of Daniel Kent, Emigrant and Redemptioner*, ed. Ella K. Bernard (Baltimore: n.p., 1904); Elizabeth Sprigs, "Elizabeth Sprigs to John Sprigs (1756)," in Isabel Calder, ed., *Colonial Captivities, Marches, and Journeys* (New York: Macmillan, 1935), 151–52. The only account that antedates William Moraley's is that of David Evans, who arrived as an indentured servant in Pennsylvania in 1704. Portions of his autobiography are printed in Boyd Stanley Schlenther, "'The English Is Swallowing Up Their Language': Welsh Ethnic Ambivalence in Colonial Pennsylvania and the Experience of David Evans," *PMHB* 114 (1990): 201–28; and in John Van Der Zee, *Bound Over: Indentured Servitude and American Conscience* (New York: Simon & Schuster, 1985), 135–45.

5. Page 64 of Moraley's autobiography as reproduced below. The page numbers of subsequent quotations from the autobiography are given in parentheses in the text.

ability to relate diverting yarns and to provide factual accounts of his own exotic travels provided him, he is convinced, with the "Reputation of an intelligent Man" (111). The autobiography concludes with a discussion of the difficulties involved in his return to England and his attempts to claim his inheritance.

Moraley narrates not only an adventure but also a morality tale, even if the message is ambiguous. His voyage through life, he hopes, illustrates that people usually bear responsibility for their own destinies. The "Calamities that afflict human Nature," Moraley advises, "are generally owing to the imprudent Management of their Affairs" (41), and "the only Way" for others to avoid difficulties like his own is "to take care how they misapply their Talents" (40). Still, according to Moraley, not all responsibility resides with the individual, since blind fate and the vagaries of fortune often determine human affairs.

The tension between these perspectives gives rise to many of Moraley's incongruities and contradictions. Birth, rank, and the authority of superiors largely decide human destiny in a more "traditional" world in which chance, external circumstance, and divine providence play significant roles. In the second, more "modern," world of the emerging bourgeoisie, individuals can, through their own intelligence, enterprise, and initiative, take advantage of freedoms and opportunities to carve out careers and to control their own lives. Regardless of his intended message, however, Moraley usually is more comfortable in the hierarchical world of birthright, familial connections, and inheritance. Rather than declaring that he is the master of his life, Moraley proclaims himself the "Tennis-ball of Fortune" (108). This is not the young Franklin who wants not only to be "in *reality* industrious and frugal, but [also] to avoid all *appearance* of the contrary."[6] Moraley hopes to prosper by inheriting his parents' estate instead of by patiently pursuing the rewards of his own hard work and thrift. And while waiting for the day when wealth would be bestowed on him, he labors primarily to survive.

Like the heroes in contemporary fiction, Moraley alternates between being the didactic moralist and the unapologetic rogue. At various times a drunkard, an adventurer, a vagabond, and a petty thief, Moraley boasts that he could "rake with the best of them" (111). A smooth-talking storyteller who easily ingratiates himself with strangers, he does not hesitate to exaggerate, misrepresent his credentials, lie, and even

6. Lemisch, ed., *Benjamin Franklin*, 78–79.

briefly to renounce his otherwise strong Anglican faith. He certainly lacks that concern for prudent behavior, often associated with the middle class, which equates morality with fiscal responsibility. Moraley wastes his parents' money, fritters away his opportunities, avoids paying his debts, breaks contracts with his employers, imposes on his friends, and defrauds his betrothed of a gold ring. He saves one woman from drowning but subsequently encourages and accepts repeated payments for his deed. He helps another woman and her children find their way along a lonely road but takes credit for not being "uncivil" to her during the night.

Yet compared with the cruelties and gratuitous violence presented in many rogue tales of the day, Moraley makes a very tame, respectable, even domesticated scoundrel. He neither pursues the utter ruin of innocent victims, nor does he torture, murder, or rape. He absconds and rebels only when he feels his parents, masters, and employers have already broken their compacts with him (a defense that would serve the colonists well in 1776), and he pilfers primarily to eat or to win the acceptance of his companions. A purloined ring finances a night of drunken carousing with his friends, some stolen geese provide fresh food for his shipmates on their homeward journey, and several pounds of embezzled raisins supplement a meager diet on the voyage to America. Moraley's charm is as evident as his blemishes in his memoirs, and his portrayal of his own ambivalent character makes the tale all the more human and delightful.

Moraley's autobiography not only tells an entertaining story but it contains much that is of historical value. We have reproduced it with very few changes in order to allow Moraley to speak with his own voice and to encourage readers themselves to enjoy and evaluate the tale and thereby to act as their own historians. Chapter headings designed for a nineteenth-century abridged reprinting have been included for ease of reading and reference, a few obvious typographical errors have been corrected, and the use of the British pound sign (£) has been modernized. Otherwise, spelling, punctuation, grammar, and emphasis are as they appeared in the original 1743 version.[7]

7. The *Delaware County Republican* (Chester, Pa.) reprinted the abridged version of Moraley's autobiography in 1884, an edition of which survives in the Historical Society of Pennsylvania. We have printed the complete and original version of the memoirs available at the William L. Clements Library, University of Michigan, Ann Arbor. See Appendix A for the autobiography's publication history.

The documentation of Moraley's autobiography is particularly important because imaginary adventure tales were quite popular in England and Moraley obviously enjoyed spinning yarns.[8] He admits his pleasure at "wonderfully magnifying every Thing" (114) in describing the English king to Native Americans, and he certainly embellishes a few parts of his autobiography in a similar fashion. And, while Moraley appears in records in England, his presence in New Jersey and Pennsylvania is confirmed only by circumstantial evidence.[9]

How valid, then, is this account? The two short stories Moraley relates about Spaniards who convert to the Anglican faith are undoubtedly fictional, although they may contain some factual basis. Some of Moraley's assertions are dubious, especially his account of his trip to New York in the late summer of 1734. Here he claims to have enlisted in the British army to escape his creditors, while simultaneously serving as personal servant for a Spanish gentleman. But he returns to New Jersey without being prosecuted for desertion from the army. This all seems quite unlikely, and no other portion of Moraley's autobiography rings so false. His memoirs are otherwise subject to the same cautious reading that is required for all historical documents. Moraley commits errors in dating events (which are corrected in the footnotes), in part because he wrote a decade after the incidents he describes. Like many contemporaries in an age of faulty maps and nonexistent censuses, Moraley consistently overstates physical distance and population size. He is often gullible by modern standards. His reports of freshwater sharks in the Delaware River, of the physiology of snakes and skunks, of the origin of fossil bones, and of the upper limits of the Delaware River are examples of local lore rather than deliberate attempts to deceive.

Still, Moraley is most often a credible reporter. His memoirs are supported at many crucial points by historical sources. His birth, buri-

8. For a discussion of Daniel Defoe's influence on imaginary travel adventures, see Percy G. Adams, *Travelers and Travel Liars, 1669–1800* (Berkeley and Los Angeles: University of California Press, 1962), 105–17. See also R. W. Frantz, *The English Traveller and the Movement of Ideas, 1660–1732* (Lincoln: University of Nebraska Press, 1967).

9. Moraley was far from unique in leaving no trace in the surviving sources. Many records do not exist for this early period, in part because the primitive conditions of New Jersey and Pennsylvania discouraged recordkeeping. For example, detailed censuses, registers of the arrivals of British immigrants, city directories, and newspapers from New Jersey are not extant. Sharon Salinger found that 44 percent of male indentured servants in early Pennsylvania left no tracks in the records (*"To Serve Well and Faithfully,"* 119).

al, apprenticeship, and indenture are confirmed by ecclesiastical, guild, and public records in England. Philadelphia newspapers verify the arrival and departure of the two ships on which Moraley sailed to and from America, and advertisements offer the sale of indentured servants by the captain of the arriving vessel (see Figure 7). Moraley's depiction of scores of inhabitants of the Mid-Atlantic region likewise are accurate. These include relatively prominent people in New Jersey, such as his first master, Isaac Pearson, who was a Burlington Quaker, clockmaker, smith, assemblyman, and part owner of the Mount Holly iron foundry, as Moraley indicated; Pearson's elder daughter, Sarah; their wealthy relatives Thomas Lambert and his daughter, Hannah Lambert; the Reverend Robert Wayman, rector of St. Mary's Church; and various colonial officials. Moraley also accurately portrays less well known individuals, including Andrew Galloway, William Collum, Lawrence Holstin, and Elizabeth Paris. Moraley's account of the ghost in Pearson's home coincides with local Burlington court records, unpublished until the twentieth century. His anecdote about the witchcraft trial in Mount Holly agrees in most respects with the report published by Benjamin Franklin, although it is more than a mere summary of the newspaper article. The two wills left by Moraley's father and mother support his own account of his financial and familial difficulties. In spite of the few instances of imaginative license, Moraley's own judgment of his work is valid: "On the Whole, I have advanc'd nothing but what I know to be the Truth" (39).[10]

The remainder of this introduction provides background to the memoirs. After briefly reconstructing Moraley's life, we relate the autobiography to the literary developments of the era, especially the evolution of the autobiographical form and the growing popularity of adventure novels. Moraley's career is scrutinized with regard to that of

10. Records of Moraley's birth and baptism, apprenticeship, and burial are cited below in footnotes 11, 14, and 19, respectively. The advertisement offering indentured servants for sale is reproduced in Figure 7. The footnotes to Moraley's autobiography contain the citations for his indenture (chap. 1, n. 17); for the arrival and departure of the ships that carried Moraley to and from Philadelphia (chap. 3, n. 8 [see also Figure 7] and chap. 10, n. 9, respectively); for Isaac Pearson (chap. 3, n. 11); for Sarah Pearson (chap. 5, n. 1); for residents of the Burlington area (chap. 5, nn. 3–7; chap. 7; nn. 22, 27; chap. 8, nn. 13, 14, 16); and for colonial officials (chap. 7, nn. 12, 16; chap. 8, n. 18). The legend about the ghost in Pearson's house is discussed in Appendix G; reports about the witchcraft "trial" are reprinted in Appendix H; and the wills of Moraley's father and mother are reproduced in Appendix C.

Benjamin Franklin and in connection with the limitations Moraley's occupations imposed on his own material success. We conclude by considering the author's social, political, and religious worlds. Throughout this introduction, we identify a host of issues and paradoxes about eighteenth-century life that William Moraley's account raises, a number of which remain open to differing interpretations.

The Life of William Moraley

Despite his assertions about the wealth and social standing of the London family into which he was born on February 25, 1699, William Moraley hailed from a modest background. His memoirs detail the family pedigree but do not identify his paternal grandfather, a curious omission given Moraley's concern with lineage. While Moraley claims to be allied to various noble families, his connections are remote and tenuous. Moreover, he fails to note that at the time of his own birth his father still worked as a journeyman clockmaker, a position he would occupy for another fourteen years.[11] According to Moraley, his father's eldest brother had wasted the family fortune, forcing his father to seek his own livelihood. Even though burdened with a young family as a journeyman, Moraley's father prospered as he reached the upper ranks of

11. The son of William Moraley and Martha Mason Moraley, William Moraley was born on February 25, 1699, and baptized four days later. (Throughout this introduction we have converted all years from the old style calendar to the new style.) Moraley's father initially had been apprenticed on February 8, 1680. He briefly served two masters, Henry Child and Philip Corderoy, before completing a term of seven years under Thomas Tompion, a renowned clock and watchmaker who is credited with several major innovations in the craft. He achieved his freedom in 1688 after having served for eight years learning the art and mystery of clockmaking. He worked for Tompion as a journeyman until Tompion's death in 1713. The office of the Archbishop of Canterbury in Knightrider Street, London, issued the marriage license for Moraley's parents on November 24, 1697. Moraley's birth and baptism are recorded in Willoughby A. Littledale, ed., *The Registers of Christ Church, Newgate, 1538 to 1754*, vol. 21 of *Publications of the Harleian Society—Registers*, 105 vols. (London: Harleian Society, 1895), 91. The apprenticeship of Moraley's father is recorded in Charles Edward Atkins, *Register of Apprentices of the Worshipful Company of Clockmakers of the City of London from Its Incorporation in 1631 to Its Tercentenary in 1931* (Privately printed, 1931), 203. The date of the marriage license of Moraley's parents is in George E. Cokayne and Edward Alexander Fry, eds., *The Index Library: Calendar of Marriage Licenses Issued by the Faculty Office, 1632–1714* (London: By subscription, 1905), 153.

the artisan class, perhaps aided in his career by his father-in-law, a "wealthy Founder and Citizen" (42).[12]

Moraley blames his parents' "over Indulgence" of their only child for having "laid the Foundation of all the Evils that have since befallen me" (43). By his own account, William squandered his early academic and vocational opportunities. "Being of too lively a Disposition" and "always preferring the present Time to the future" (43), he did not take advantage of his respectable education in Latin, arithmetic, the fine arts, and natural philosophy. As an attorney's clerk, he failed to study the law and instead "did little else but vapour about the Streets" (45) of London. Moraley's profligate ways would haunt him periodically for the rest of his life. A friend of the family recalled many years later that Moraley was a good-natured spendthrift "whose wants were few and cares, less."[13] Disappointed by his son's lackadaisical approach to his career, and disgruntled with the law as a profession, Moraley's father removed him from his clerkship and a year or two later, in 1718, personally took him on as an apprentice to instruct him in the art and mystery of watchmaking.[14]

Before Moraley completed his apprenticeship, his father lost a substantial investment when stock in the South Sea Company collapsed in 1720. The family moved to Newcastle-upon-Tyne in an effort to recoup their fortune. About that time, Moraley and his father became alienated for unstated reasons. William claims that he was now "tractable, and obedient to my Father's Commands" (46), but he also admits to having made "ill Use" (52) of his parents' support through the mismanagement of his affairs. By 1725 Moraley's father had rewritten his will, leaving only 20 shillings and some watchmaker's tools to his son. When, shortly thereafter, the senior Moraley died unexpectedly, the estrangement became fixed by testamentary law. William's mother, Martha, was more inclined to assist her son than her husband had been, and she

12. G. H. Baillie, C. Clutton, and C. A. Ilbert, *Britten's Old Clocks and Watches and Their Makers* (New York: Dutton, 1956), 441.

13. Manuscript sheet tipped into the Clements Library copy of Moraley's autobiography and attributed to Thomas Bell. See Appendix A.

14. The precise timing of these events is unclear. Moraley states that he became a clerk at the age of fifteen—in 1714 or 1715—and that he continued in that position for nearly two years. But he did not officially enter into apprenticeship to his father (which he apparently never completed) until May 5, 1718 (Atkins, *Register of Apprentices*, 204).

gave him £20 instead of the 20 shillings stipulated in the will. But Martha Moraley had little money of her own, and she was constrained initially by the provisions of the will and subsequently by her remarriage. Despite continual quarrels with his mother about the inheritance, young William could wheedle only 12 additional shillings from her when he set out for London in 1728 to "seek my Fortune" (48).

When Moraley could not find work in London he quickly fell on hard times. He blamed his father's will, his mother, and himself for his woes. Unlike Benjamin Franklin and many other eighteenth-century artisans, Moraley seems throughout his life to have had little understanding of the financial cycles that adversely affected him. That England suffered an economic contraction between 1728 and 1731 appears not to have occurred to him as a reason for his difficulties.[15] Moraley failed to record that he was imprisoned for debt and then released under the Insolvent Debtor's Act on May 31, 1729.[16] Facing poverty and even starvation, Moraley sold himself three months later—at the relatively advanced age of thirty—for a five-year stint as a bound servant in the "American Plantations" (50).

The ship *Boneta*, carrying a cargo of Moraley and other indentured servants, cleared customs in early September and, after brief stops along the English coast, sailed for the colonies. After an uneventful but eye-opening voyage, the vessel docked in Philadelphia, where Isaac Pearson, a clockmaker living in nearby Burlington, New Jersey, purchased Moraley. William spent the following three years in Pearson's household. Here he repaired clocks and watches, sweated over a smith's forge, herded livestock, toiled in an iron foundry, and performed other miscellaneous jobs. But before his term was completed, Moraley became disgruntled. He wanted to serve the remainder of his bondage in Philadelphia, which he describes as "one of the most delightful Cities upon Earth" (64). When Pearson refused consent, Moraley absconded but was quickly apprehended. Philadelphia's mayor mediated the dispute between master and servant, convincing Pearson to forgive two years' service and quieting Moraley's restlessness. Under the circumstances Moraley was extremely fortunate, because servants who fled could legally

15. John J. McCusker and Russell R. Menard summarize the studies of English business cycles in *The Economy of British America, 1607–1789* (Chapel Hill: University of North Carolina Press, 1985), 62–64.

16. *London Gazette*, no. 6782, May 31, 1729.

have their terms of servitude extended to compensate their masters for the lost time and expense of recovering their human property.[17]

After successfully completing his indenture, Moraley roamed around the colonies from New York to Maryland for about twenty months, seeking employment, looking for adventure, visiting relatives, and taking refuge from his creditors. He initially moved to Philadelphia, where he indented himself to a watchmaker, Edmund Lewis. But Lewis proved to be a shiftless master, too fond of alcohol to support his servant, so Moraley departed and subsequently worked as a journeyman for another newly arrived watchmaker, William Graham. When this employer left three months later to seek greater opportunity in the Caribbean, Moraley was left unemployed and forced to wander the streets, sleep in suburban barns, and borrow money and food from his friends and acquaintances. He callously courted and became engaged to an older woman whose scrap metal business afforded him the opportunity to become a property owner, but he squandered this chance when he allowed his friends to steal the gold ring given him by his betrothed.

Once again reduced to poverty and near starvation, Moraley decided to travel the country circuit, cleaning timepieces and working as a tinsmith, although he had no training in the latter occupation. While he generally met with warm hospitality during his rambles, his desultory employment and his fear of the wilderness dampened his enthusiasm for an itinerant existence. Moraley lost his way in dark forests along unmarked roads and was frightened by wild beasts, misled by mockingbirds, and apprehended as a runaway servant by bounty hunters. These rustic adventures overwhelmed an urbanite like Moraley, who preferred his encounters with nature to be "Romantick" (85) rather than intimidating. He consequently settled down for six weeks as a black-

17. New Jersey law stipulated that escaped servants were to serve two extra days for each day they were absent, and the courts could add additional time to compensate masters for expenses incurred in capturing runaways (Smith, *Colonists in Bondage*, 267). Moraley's master, Isaac Pearson, might have absolved Moraley of two years' service in return for his agreement not to abscond again, or it may be related to the concurrent rebuke of Pearson by the Burlington Monthly Meeting for "walking disorderly"—that is, for behavior that was not in accordance with the strict precepts of the Society of Friends. The local meeting accepted Pearson's handwritten apology on March 2, 1730, two months after Moraley took up residence in the household. It is possible that Pearson had driven too hard a bargain in his purchase of Moraley—£11 for five years' service—and his subsequent forgiveness of part of Moraley's servitude may have been mandated by the meeting. See Minutes of the Burlington Monthly Meeting, Microfilm, March 2, 1730, Burlington County Historical Society, Burlington, New Jersey.

smith in Burlington. Moraley claims that when his Philadelphia creditors located him he fled briefly to New York, where he found employment both as a personal servant and as a soldier. He soon returned to Burlington to work again at the blacksmith's shop.

Discouraged about his prospects in America and heartened by the possibility that his mother's third marriage might provide an opportunity to obtain part of her estate, Moraley decided to return to England. He made an agreement with a ship's captain to work for his passage as a cook on board a vessel bound for Ireland. Before the ship sailed, Moraley took a three-week trip to Maryland to visit his mother's relative, during which time he had more adventures. Returning to the ship, Moraley hid aboard from his creditors while the vessel was docked in Philadelphia, and he narrowly escaped a former employer's attempt to reclaim him for failing to fulfill the terms of his contract. Moraley breathed much easier once the ship was under full sail in the early autumn of 1734.[18]

The journey home proved arduous. The Atlantic voyage was long, and the connection from Ireland to England was difficult. Moraley finally landed at Workington on December 26, 1734, in a filthy condition, wearing rags, and without a penny in his pocket—not much different from the way he had left his homeland five years earlier. He walked eighty miles, mostly through pouring rain during the next nine days, and depended on the charity of strangers for food and shelter. After numerous trials he arrived home to a warm reception befitting a prodigal son and lived with his mother until her death three years later.

His tale ends with an account of more financial difficulties. William's mother distrusted her son's profligate character and specified in her will

18. Moraley remembered the date his ship sailed incorrectly. It probably left on September 25 rather than July 25. According to reports in the city's newspapers, the *Sea Flower*, commanded by Oswald Peel, cleared the port of Philadelphia for Dublin during the week of September 19–26, 1734. This date corresponds to Moraley's other observations. First, he notes that at least a month before sailing he helped harvest the corn in the area around Burlington, which would not have been ripe until early September. Second, he indicates that he arrived in England on December 26, after an approximate three-month ocean voyage, meaning that his ship probably embarked from America in late September. Third, Moraley states that, on arriving in England, he had worn the same shirt for fourteen or fifteen weeks, a shirt purchased several weeks before both his three-week trip to Maryland and the Atlantic crossing. The *Sea Flower*, commanded by Oswald Peel, entered Philadelphia's port between June 27 and July 4, 1734, according to newspaper sources. After unloading its cargo from Barbados, it probably proceeded to Burlington to load staves, then returned to Philadelphia before sailing for Ireland. See the *Pennsylvania Gazette* (Philadelphia) and the *American Weekly Mercury* (Philadelphia), June 27–July 4 and September 19–September 26 issues.

that the three executors of her estate should liquidate her assets and purchase an annuity from which to dispense a monthly allowance to her son for the rest of his life. Disappointed once again in his inheritance, Moraley rails against the "mistakes" committed by the executors. His memoirs conclude by emphasizing that, although obliged "to follow the meanest Imploy for a Subsistance" (142), he is resigned "to the Will of Providence" (143). The details of his later life are nebulous. Apparently he worked as a watchmaker in Newcastle, where he died and was buried in St. Nicholas churchyard on January 9, 1762.[19]

Moraley's Autobiography and Contemporary Literature

Moraley never explains why he wrote his memoirs, although the hope of making money was a likely motivating factor. Biographies and autobiographies, both fictional and factual, had recently enjoyed enormous success in England. The translation of numerous sensational French memoirs attracted particular note early in the eighteenth century, while writers like Daniel Defoe and Jonathan Swift helped create a new audience for exciting adventure tales about such figures as Robinson Crusoe, Moll Flanders, and Lemuel Gulliver.[20] Assessing these developments, Moraley published his autobiography at his own expense, probably hoping that the proceeds from its sale would solve his continuing fiscal problems. His chances of making a profit, however, were slight.

In addition, Moraley may have wished publicly to explain his problems to his neighbors and to plea for their sympathy. The narrative's conclusion notes his intention to "endeavour to perswade the World to have a better Opinion of me" (142). Moraley also may have wanted to thank his supporters and creditors and to chastise his enemies. He promised Humphrey Senhouse, who had given him aid, "to write to

19. M. A. Richardson, *The Local Historian's Table Book, of Remarkable Occurrences, Historical Facts, Traditions, Legendary and Descriptive Ballads, etc., etc., Connected with the Counties of Newcastle-upon-Tyne, Northumberland and Durham*, 8 vols. (Newcastle-upon-Tyne: Richardson, 1841), 2:104.

20. Wayne Shumaker, *English Autobiography: Its Emergence, Materials, and Form* (Berkeley and Los Angeles: University of California Press, 1954), 60–61; Donald A. Stauffer, *The Art of Biography in Eighteenth-Century England*, 2 vols. (Princeton: Princeton University Press, 1941), 1:77, 135.

him when I got home" (136), and the memoirs may represent a belated fulfillment of that pledge to Senhouse and others. Still, Moraley's expression of gratitude in the preface to the "Worthy Gentlemen of *Newcastle*" (39) is ambivalent. On the one hand, he may sincerely have been acknowledging them "for the many Favours they have bestow'd on me" (39), including bailing him out of jail. On the other hand, he might have been sarcastically lambasting the executors who impeded his inheritance of his mother's property since he had "no other Way to retaliate them" (39).[21] Moraley returns to the latter theme in his closing pages, remarking pointedly that his own hardships were "infinitely preferrable to an Estate got by illegal Means" (143).

Current literature helped shape Moraley's interpretation of his life, and it is only natural that his memoirs would be influenced by the literary styles of his time. Like many contemporary autobiographers, he adopted the popular fashion of personally narrated adventure stories, which often blended the fantastic with the authentic.[22] Olaudah Equiano, an enslaved African living in the Atlantic world, and Benjamin Franklin both modeled their memoirs on earlier spiritual narratives and employed the techniques of contemporary picaresque fiction to depict their own lives.[23] But like Equiano and Franklin, Moraley's use of established rhetorical devices does not mean that he generally sacrificed accuracy in his description of life, and the manuscript's historical validity is not destroyed by his occasional use of hyperbole. Indeed, despite his stylized approach, Moraley appears to have been much more honest than Franklin in rendering his own character.

21. Moraley may have purposely created the ambiguity by using the word "retaliate," which had two different meanings during the early eighteenth century; it denoted repayment made in return for either an injury or a kindness (*Oxford English Dictionary* [London: Oxford University Press, 1970]).

22. Such hyperbole characterized much eighteenth-century autobiographical and fictional accounts of travel to the New World. Other books published in England near the time of Moraley's memoirs include *The Voyages and Adventures of Captain Robert Boyle . . . To which is added, The Voyage, Shipwreck, and Miraculous Preservation, of Richard Castleman, Gent. With a Description of the City of Philadelphia, and the Country of Pennsylvania* (London: Andrew Millar, 1728); and John Home, *A Journey Over Land from the Gulf of Honduras to the Great South Sea . . .* (London, 1734). Both are available in the Rare Book Room, Van Pelt Library, University of Pennsylvania, Philadelphia. Like Moraley, Castleman claims (p. 367) to have been attacked by a six-foot snake.

23. P. M. Zall, *Franklin's Autobiography: A Model Life* (Boston: Twayne Publishers, 1989), 29; Costanzo, *Surprizing Narrative*, 48–51; Henry Louis Gates Jr., "Binary Oppositions in Chapter One of *Narrative of the Life of Frederick Douglass, an American Slave, Written by Himself*," in *Afro-American Literature: The Reconstruction of Instruction*, ed. Dexter Fisher and Robert B. Stepto (New York: Modern Language Association of America, 1978), 214.

Depicting himself as a picaresque hero, Moraley wrote in a well-established genre stretching from sixteenth-century Spanish writers to Elizabethan authors to such eighteenth-century novelists as Defoe and Swift. In their journeys from place to place, picaros sought adventures that would contribute both to their increasing awareness of the world and to their maturity. One primary purpose of these stories was to entertain. Using this approach, Moraley diverted readers with tales not only about himself but also about other people's exotic travels and their dangerous and thrilling escapades.[24] As part of a rhetorical strategy designed to capture the reader's imagination, Moraley enlivened his autobiography with three lengthy digressions that recount the sagas of "George Sonds's Two Sons" (chapter 2), "The Fortunate Andalousian" (chapter 4), and "The Valentian" (chapter 9).

Personal accounts of travel, both nonfictional and fictional, enjoyed immense popularity in eighteenth-century England. William Dampier's *New Voyage Round the World* of 1697, Captain Cook's *Voyages*, and John Green's *New General Collection of Voyages and Travels, the World Display'd* were three best-sellers credited with reviving travel literature. An important component of this genre was its emphasis on the physical voyage through sometimes "bizarre" regions of the world as constituting a vital spiritual journey as well. The education gained through daily experience aided the evolution of the protagonist's moral consciousness. Of equal relevance are the novels of Daniel Defoe, especially *Robinson Crusoe*, a work that undoubtedly influenced Moraley, since at one point he compared himself to its hero (133). Like Crusoe, Moraley expressed his wonder in discovering curious new objects and unfamiliar life in foreign lands. Moraley also provided a wealth of observations and minute details about the flora, fauna, and inhabitants of the New World, much as Crusoe described his island.[25]

Moraley's memoirs can be understood as part of the evolution of the autobiographical form. The religious introspection that characterized

24. Raymond Hedrin, "The American Slave Narrative: The Justification of the Picaro," *American Literature* 53 (1982): 630–45; Gates, "Binary Oppositions," 214; and Costanzo, *Surprizing Narrative*, chap. 4.

25. Peter N. Skrine, *The Baroque: Literature and Culture in Seventeenth-Century Europe* (New York: Holmes & Meier, 1978), 70–71; Costanzo, *Surprizing Narrative*, 48–49; Monroe Z. Hafter, "Toward a History of Spanish Imaginary Voyages," *Eighteenth-Century Studies* 8 (Spring 1975): 265–82; and Martin Green, *The Robinson Crusoe Story* (University Park: The Pennsylvania State University Press, 1990), chap. 2.

the seventeenth century, especially as fostered by such sects as the Puritans and the Quakers, produced a number of personal histories. George Fox and John Woolman were among the many Quakers who kept journals as a means of self-evaluation designed to aid their understanding of their own "inner light" and their relationship with God. Other religious authors wrote memoirs depicting their fall from grace and subsequent redemption, thereby providing models that readers might emulate in their private struggles for salvation. English autobiographies became increasingly secular during the eighteenth century. Some American authors, most notably Benjamin Franklin, depicted strongly individualistic characters committed primarily to achieving personal material success and, on occasion, to serving humankind; rarely were these men overwhelmed with a sense of urgency to realize spiritual salvation. In addition, adventurous and observant memoirs grew more numerous and popular, paralleling in many respects the simultaneous evolution of the novel. Yet it is important to note that even though the form of autobiographies and novels developed contemporaneously and in a similar fashion, autobiographies did not necessarily contain fictional passages.[26]

Moraley's account is a secularized version of the early religious autobiographers who chronicled their fall from grace and their struggle for redemption. In a parallel to the biblical parable of the prodigal son (to which he twice refers), Moraley loses parental providence when his father dies and his mother rejects him. His departure from his "earthly paradise" takes him into the "real world" of travel and adventure, where life is governed more by fate and chance than by God's omnipotent will. Cast into a lowly position in the American colonies, Moraley contends against the vicissitudes of fortune for five years before finally being redeemed by returning to his mother and the physical comfort of her estate.

The theme of the conflicting relationships between parents and children permeates the memoirs. Moraley's deep ambivalence about both his father and his mother characterizes the story not only of his own life but also of all the tales he relates: George Sonds and his two sons, the two Spanish gentlemen and their fathers, and the woman who returned from Charleston to her father in Ireland. Moraley's concern was hardly

26. On the parallel development of novels and autobiographies, see Shumaker, *English Autobiography*, 5, 20–30; Margaret Bottrall, *Every Man a Phoenix: Studies in Seventeenth-Century Autobiography* (London: William Clowes & Sons, 1958), 4, 141–44, 161–62; and Costanzo, *Surprizing Narrative*, 49–51.

unique. The eighteenth century was a crucial era of changing relationships between parents and offspring throughout the English world. Among the upper classes in particular, authoritarian parents who rigidly enforced obedience and dependence in their children were being replaced by indulgent parents who valued the individuality of their offspring within a sentimental, loving relationship.[27]

Moraley's memoirs belong principally to the secular tradition of autobiography. His fundamental concern throughout the writing of his memoirs was to obtain the inheritance of his family's estate and thereby to secure a materially comfortable life. But he still employed some techniques of spiritual autobiography by offering readers a moral lesson on the importance of individual responsibility and advising people to improve their "Talents" and to manage their affairs prudently. But Moraley, in contrast to many fictional and nonfictional characters, never really learned to apply his own lesson. Crusoe found that deliverance from sin was more important than deliverance from his island, Gulliver discovered the need to exercise the lessons of virtue he had learned, and Franklin ascertained how to fashion his character to accomplish his purposes. Moraley, however, neither developed his talents nor assumed full responsibility for his own misfortunes.[28] Instead, he concluded his memoirs by whining about having to work for a living at "the meanest Imploy" (142) and by railing at the executors of his mother's estate.

Benjamin Franklin, Social Mobility, and Moraley's Career

Moraley's life affords a valuable comparison to the myth and the reality of the first great American hero, Benjamin Franklin. Both Moraley and Franklin arrived in Philadelphia during the 1720s as "marginal" men

27. See, e.g., Lawrence Stone, *The Family, Sex, and Marriage in England, 1500–1800* (New York: Harper & Row, 1977); and Steven Mintz and Susan Kellogg, *Domestic Revolutions: A Social History of American Family Life* (New York: The Free Press, 1988). Similar changes in the family occurred among working Philadelphians during the second half of the eighteenth century; see Billy G. Smith, *The "Lower Sort": Philadelphia's Laboring People, 1750–1800* (Ithaca, N.Y.: Cornell University Press, 1990), chap. 7.

28. Edwin B. Benjamin, "Symbolic Elements in Robinson Crusoe," *Philological Quarterly* 30 (October 1951): 207; Donald Greene, "The Education of Lemuel Gulliver," in Peter Hughes and David Williams, eds., *The Varied Pattern: Studies in the Eighteenth Century*, vol. 1 (Toronto: A. M. Hakkert, 1971), 13–14; Costanzo, *Surprizing Narrative*, 50–51.

embarrassed by their appearance. Attired in an old red coat, coarse checkered shirt, bad shoes, and a dirty wig, Moraley was a bound servant waiting to be purchased. Franklin was a runaway apprentice who wore dirty work clothes and had his "pockets stuffed out with shirts and stockings." Both men spent their last three pennies to buy bread and then walked around town. Thereafter, their first hours in the city diverged sharply, according to their reminiscences. Franklin gave his left-over bread to a friendless woman and child, attended a Quaker meeting, and sought out a reputable inn for lodging; the next day he applied for work. Moraley sold his clothes to buy rum and cider and amused himself by revising George Webb's poem about Philadelphia and later by pretending it was his own composition. While Moraley praised the city's "many Houses of Entertainment" (68) where evening drinkers enjoyed the "Product of this fertile Soil" (68), Franklin discovered "young people of the town that were lovers of reading, with whom I spent my evenings very pleasantly and gained money by my industry and frugality."[29]

Moraley and Franklin may well have met, because both traveled frequently between Burlington and Philadelphia during the early 1730s. Franklin remembered Isaac Pearson, Moraley's master, as one of several Burlington Quakers who was "of great use to me, as I occasionally was to some of them." And Pearson's house stood just four doors from the print shop Franklin used in Burlington. Moraley's lengthy discussion of colonial paper-currency policy and the process of printing money reflects Franklin's contemporary interests. Moraley's ideas on this topic exhibit an economic sophistication that is not otherwise apparent in his memoirs, although they are more than mere copies of Franklin's pamphlet advocating a more liberal currency policy. Moraley also confirms Franklin's newspaper story about the trial by "swimming" of two suspected witches in Mount Holly, New Jersey, in 1730, an account which many scholars have dismissed as a hoax (see Appendix H).[30]

The two artisans shared a few character traits and professed some similar values. Both hoped to be ingratiating by shaping their behavior to gain influence over others and to build their reputation. Franklin "made it a rule to forbear all direct contradiction to the sentiments of others and all positive assertions of my own," while Moraley took pride

29. Lemisch, ed., *Benjamin Franklin*, 38–41 (quotation from p. 41).
30. Ibid., 69.

in his ability to "change my Note as proper Time offer'd" (111). Both men defined success in material terms, and both celebrated the centrality of the individual through the autobiographical form. Like Franklin, Moraley also worked hard, on occasion, and he took pride in his skill and intelligence. One of his moments of despair occurred when he was asked to split logs but failed miserably. Some instruction, however, enabled him "to acquit Myself manfully" and to "my own Satisfaction" (124). Franklin more obviously rewrote his character in his memoirs, depicting himself as the model of the emerging middle-class morality. Still, he recorded that the newly employed young printer, not unlike Moraley, spent his first scarce cash on such luxuries as fine clothes and a watch.[31]

Fundamental differences also separated the two men. By their own accounts, Franklin experienced "constant good fortune," while Moraley was the "most unfortunate of Mankind" (40). Franklin achieved incredible personal success that captured the imagination of contemporaries at home and abroad. His fame and his promotion of hard work and frugality helped define the trajectory of social mobility basic to the "American dream." The mythical Franklin, like the fictional Crusoe, represented the new eighteenth-century capitalist entrepreneurs who believed they could shape their own destiny.[32]

Moraley, meanwhile, remained primarily a traditionalist. Unable fully to enter the ranks of the middling sort, he struggled instead merely to make ends meet, an experience not uncommon among freed servants. Moraley's financial failure derives from several sources. Conditions in the Mid-Atlantic region were not particularly favorable for watchmakers, and Moraley could not easily adopt a new occupation since his skills were not readily transferable to other crafts. As a committed urbanite, he had little interest in and no talent for farming, the vocation of the vast majority of male residents of the middle colonies. Moreover, like many artisans, he envisioned himself ultimately as a master craftsman, although it was a goal to be achieved by inheriting necessary funds rather than by dedicating himself to years of toil and thrift, like Franklin. The careers of neither man can be described as "typical," nor can their stories settle the continuing historical debate about the extent of social mobility in early America. But Moraley's tale

31. Ibid., 43–44 (quotation from p. 104).

32. Ibid. (quotation from p. 16). See also Green, *Robinson Crusoe*, 21–24.

provides insights into the lives of thousands of migrants who achieved, at best, modest material success, became a part of the itinerant poor, or eventually returned to their native country.[33]

Moraley provides a mixed assessment of the material conditions and economic opportunities available in the middle colonies. On the one hand, he repeats the shibboleths of European travelers by declaring the Mid-Atlantic region "the best poor Man's Country" (89), where "the richest Farmers in the World" (93) bask in "Affluence and Plenty" (93).[34] On the other hand, he recognizes that not everyone shared this abundance. An essential source of the wealth of many landowners, Moraley explains, was that they purchased servants and slaves rather than paying wages for labor, a system that helped enrich independent farmers but often did not serve bound workers particularly well.

Moraley characterizes the condition of servants as "very hard" (96) and that of slaves as "very bad" (94). He contends that earlier in the history of the middle colonies, when European servants received land as part of their freedom dues, they enjoyed relatively good opportunities to prosper after their servitude. But by the time of his own bondage, conditions had changed significantly. Because real estate was no longer distributed to servants at the conclusion of their indenture, the possibility of advancement from servant to property owner was considerably more remote. By Moraley's time, the most valuable farms in southeastern Pennsylvania had been claimed, forcing the "poorer sort," according to historian James T. Lemon, to move "beyond the limits of settlement and speculative holdings" if they hoped to obtain real estate.[35] Thus, reflecting on his decision to sign an indenture to America, Moraley "curs'd my Fate ten thousand times" (54). And once free of his servitude yet unable to fulfill his personal aspirations, Moraley "resolv'd to embrace the first Opportunity" (124) to return to England. Both Moraley's

33. The historical literature debating the extent of social mobility in early America is vast. Two recent accounts that differ in their assessments of the opportunities available to freed servants are Salinger, *"To Serve Well and Faithfully"*; and Galenson, *White Servitude in Colonial America*.

34. For similar sentiments, see Christopher Sauer, "An Early Description of Pennsylvania: Letter of Christopher Sauer Written in 1724, Describing Conditions in Philadelphia and Vicinity, and the Sea Voyage from Europe," ed. Rayner W. Kelsey, trans. Adolph Gerber, *PMHB* 45 (1921): 249; Patrick M'Roberts, "Patrick M'Roberts' Tour Through a Part of the Northern Provinces of America," ed. Carl Bridenbaugh, *PMHB* 59 (1935): 136; Joseph Poultney to Robert Dixon, December 15, 1783, "A Letter of Joseph Poultney," *PMHB* 52 (1928): 95.

35. James T. Lemon, *The Best Poor Man's Country: A Geographical Study of Early Southeastern Pennsylvania* (New York: Norton, 1972), 68.

analysis of the prospects of servants and his personal experience lend support to recent arguments of scholars who have detected a narrowing of economic opportunities in the middle colonies during the eighteenth century, especially for men without property or skills in high demand.[36]

Like at least half of European emigrants to North America during the eighteenth century, Moraley signed a contract called an indenture. This was an agreement by an emigrant to work as a servant for a designated master for a period of years—usually three or four—in return for the cost of the Atlantic passage, daily maintenance, and, perhaps, freedom dues at the conclusion of their term. Slightly more than half of all indentured servants in the eighteenth century were young men between sixteen and twenty years of age who either claimed no occupational skills or were experienced farmers. The servants who were skilled artisans tended to be somewhat older. Scholars have long speculated about the various forces that impelled people to sell themselves into bondage. Moraley's own decision was based primarily on "push" factors out of the Old World rather than on "pull" factors to the New World. Battered by unemployment, poverty, imprisonment for debt, the slim chance of obtaining a substantial sum from his mother, and the lack of any "Prospect of advancing myself" (52) in London, Moraley was fatalistic, "not caring what became of me" (50–51) or where he went. His motivation to sign an indenture to Pennsylvania thus grew more out of desperation about his condition in England than out of a positive vision of his chances in America.[37]

A brief period of peace on the high seas, famine in Ireland, war in Germany, and economic difficulties in England all encouraged Moraley and thousands of others to emigrate to the New World in the late 1720s and the 1730s. Approximately 73,000 Europeans traveled to British North America during the 1730s, nearly twice as many as the average

36. Salinger, *"To Serve Well and Faithfully."* But see also Paul G. E. Clemens and Lucy Simler, "Rural Labor and the Farm Household in Chester County, Pennsylvania, 1750–1820," in Stephen Innes, ed., *Work and Labor in Early America* (Chapel Hill: University of North Carolina Press, 1988), 106–43; and Lucy Simler, "The Landless Worker: An Index of Economic and Social Change in Chester County, Pennsylvania, 1750–1820," *PMHB* 114 (1990): 163–200. Clemens and Simler argue that propertyless men in southeastern Pennsylvania were able to employ various strategies to improve their economic position. On the limited advancement opportunities of poorer Philadelphians, see Smith, *The "Lower Sort,"* chap. 5.

37. Various explanations of motivations of indentured servants are offered by Salinger, *"To Serve Well and Faithfully"*; Galenson, *White Servitude in Colonial America*; Grubb, "Redemptioner Immigration to Pennsylvania"; and Grubb, "The Market for Indentured Immigrants."

during each of the century's first three decades. With its temperate climate and generally healthy economy, the Delaware River valley was an attractive destination; at least 17,000 migrants arrived in Philadelphia's port in the 1730s. The plight of immigrants was shifting as poorer people now accounted for a larger proportion of the new arrivals. Nearly one of every three passengers disembarking in Philadelphia during the 1730s was an indentured servant, and they were joined by an additional five hundred slaves.[38]

To appreciate better the opportunities and limitations Moraley encountered in both England and America, we need to examine his occupational history in some detail. The artisan world in which Moraley operated consisted of three tiers: apprentices, journeymen, and masters. Ideally, artisans made steady progress during their careers, moving from apprentice to journeyman to master of their craft. A young boy usually served for between four and ten years as an apprentice, and, in return for his unpaid labor, he received instruction in the basic skills, daily maintenance, and often a small gift of clothes or tools from his master at the end of his apprenticeship. A journeyman hired out for wages to a master but generally owned his own tools. He might labor for a number of years in that status, waiting to accumulate both the capital and the additional skills necessary to establish himself as a master. Only a master was independent, typically working for himself out of his home. He was free to marry, establish his own household, and hire journeymen and take on apprentices as assistants.

This ideal career frequently did not match reality. Even in William Hogarth's rendering of the supremely successful career (see Figures 1, 2,

38. The number of immigrants is drawn from Henry A. Gemery, "Disarray in the Historical Record: Estimates of Immigration to the United States, 1700–1860," in Klepp, ed., *Demographic History*, table 1, p. 126; Klepp, "Demography in Early Philadelphia, 1690–1860," ibid., table 4, p. 111; Jean R. Soderlund, "Black Importation and Migration into Southeastern Pennsylvania, 1682–1810," ibid., table 1, p. 146; Wokeck, "German and Irish Immigration to Colonial Philadelphia," ibid., 128–43; and Darold W. Wax, "The Negro Slave Trade in Colonial Pennsylvania" (Ph.D. diss., University of Washington, 1962), table 1, p. 46, table 2, p. 48. The changing character of the immigrants is from Salinger, *"To Serve Well and Faithfully,"* 47–60, 178. For 1729, the year Moraley landed, there is an unusually detailed tally of arrivals at the port of Philadelphia: 267 English and Welsh passengers arrived, of whom 68 were indentured servants; 1,155 Irish passengers arrived, of whom 230 were servants; 43 servants from Scotland arrived; and 243 Palantines arrived as paying passengers. An additional 4,500 passengers, most of whom were from Ireland, landed in Delaware (John Oldmixon, *The British Empire in America* [London, 1741], 321).

and 3), hard work and thrift did not bring a slow and steady accumulation of capital. Instead, hard work gained the industrious apprentice a good reputation, and his reward was the hand of his master's daughter and partnership in an established enterprise. Rather than earning independence in his own right, the fortunate apprentice would be endowed with capital by his social superiors through familial channels. Thus, some journeymen with access to capital became masters even though they possessed few skills, while others, like Moraley, remained wage earners for their entire lives no matter how hard they labored.

Moraley's economic story begins with considerable promise for success. William was fifteen years old in 1714 when his father bound him as a clerk to an attorney. This was an expensive undertaking; his father probably paid the lawyer between £150 and £200 to take his son as a clerk and teach him law. But success in that profession required more than money. The "Professor of this Science," according to a contemporary career handbook, "must not be born a Blockhead; he must have a clear, solid, and unclouded Understanding, a distinguishing Head, and a puzzling, unpuzzled Brain." In addition, the clerk should be a "Gentleman born" and liberally educated. William Moraley had been provided with a pedigree and had studied—if in a lackadaisical fashion—Latin, history, theology, arithmetic, and science. But because he came from the middling rather than the upper classes, Moraley may not have felt comfortable in the world of lawyers, which may partially explain why he did not apply himself or succeed as an attorney.[39]

Technically, a law clerk was a journeyman who earned a maximum wage of 10 shillings and 6 pence per week—not a high income, given the expenses of living in London. Fine clothing, a sword, and the pursuit of the "Pleasures of the Town" (45) might be heavy charges for one who was a gentleman born or who aspired to behave like one. Modest wages and high expectations caused many clerks to fall deep into debt. This combination of unsupervised adolescent clerks, a genteel ethos, and considerable financial pressure resulted, according to the career guide,

39. R. Campbell, *The London Tradesman* . . . (1747; reprint, Devon: David & Charles, 1969), quotations from 70, 71, 331. Of the 145 young men articled to attorneys in 1714, 20 percent came, like Moraley, from a middling background, 56 percent hailed from the gentry, 6 percent were from the "poorer sort," and the origins of the balance were uncertain but probably gentle (calculated from Michael Miles, "'A Haven for the Privileged': Recruitment into the Profession of Attorney in England, 1709–1792," *Social History* 11 [1986]: 197–210).

in "Cheating, Lewdness, and all manner of Debauchery being often more studied than Law or Precedents."[40]

Given the reputation of law clerks and the substantial investment in Moraley's academic education and clerkship, it is surprising that Moraley's father discovered only belatedly, in 1718, that he did not approve of the legal profession as a career for his son. An ungenerous interpretation is that Moraley Sr. withdrew his support for his son's future at a time when he was investing heavily in the South Sea Company. By removing his son from the clerkship, the father saved the expense of maintaining separate living quarters as well as the £1,000 necessary to purchase a set of chambers for the attorney-to-be.[41] Indeed, the £800 the family lost in the crash of the South Sea stock may originally have been intended to establish young William as an independent lawyer. Was it this financial transaction that prompted the senior Moraley to promise to advance his son's fortunes in exchange for adhering to parental supervision? In his autobiography, Moraley records only that his father justified his actions on moral grounds by condemning both the legal profession and his son's character. These events, however explained, are certainly one source for Moraley's deep ambivalence about parental authority.

Young William's change in status from a lawyer's clerk to a watchmaker's apprentice was substantial. In one stroke of the pen at the guild hall, the nineteen-year-old Moraley went from a profession to a trade, from journeyman to apprentice, from independence to daily subservience to his father. That the South Sea Bubble burst two years later only added to his misfortune by depleting the family's wealth.

Although watchmaking was a craft, its art was, as Adam Smith observed, "much superior to common trades."[42] A master clockmaker or watchmaker had to understand the metallurgy of brass, steel, silver, and gold; to be familiar with the crafts of the cabinetmaker, enameler, engraver, filigreemaker, jeweler, and glazier; to comprehend the me-

40. Campbell, *London Tradesman*, 72–73.

41. Ibid., 331. Moraley and his father may have considered that the apparent surplus of attorneys would make a £1,000 investment in a fledgling law practice riskier than putting the money in South Sea Company stock. Between 1712 and the market crash of 1720, some 119 new law clerks were registered each year. For the remainder of the century the annual average was less than half that number (calculated from Miles, "'A Haven for the Privileged,'" table 1, p. 199).

42. Adam Smith, *An Inquiry into the Nature and Causes of the Wealth of Nations*, 2 vols., ed. James E. Thorold Rogers (Oxford: Clarendon Press, 1869), 1:129.

chanics of wheels, pulleys, and springs, as well as the operation of the cutting and chain-making machines; and to have some comprehension of the physics of motion.[43] The apprentice should therefore possess "a Mechanic Head, [and] a light nice Hand," according to the career handbook, but "no great Strength, nor much Education" was necessary.[44] Access to the trade was more difficult than for most crafts. Apprenticeship fees ranged from £10 to £30, placing watchmaking among the most expensive 20 percent of occupations for entrance costs.[45] In London and its environs, the Clockmakers Company severely restricted the number of apprenticeships available.[46]

Between 1660 and 1775, English supremacy in clockmaking and watchmaking was unchallenged; artisans in no other country could match the skillful work, technological innovations, or low prices of London timepieces. The early appearance of many of the production and labor practices later associated with the industrial revolution created these advantages. By 1670 Thomas Tompion had introduced mass production of watches based on a system of standardized parts, an elaborate division of labor, and the subcontracting of tasks to garret shops and individual households. This efficient organization, where "*Manufactures* will beget one another," flourished in the metropolis of London. The city's artisans were soon able to specialize in the production of wheels, springs, and cases. The result, noted William Petty in 1683, was that "the *Watch* will be better and cheaper, than if the whole Work be put upon any one Man."[47]

43. M. Dorothy George, *London Life in the Eighteenth Century* (New York: Capricorn, 1965), 176; Baillie, Clutton, and Ilbert, *Britten's Old Clocks*, 270.

44. Campbell, *London Tradesman*, 252.

45. The fees charged by watchmakers and clockmakers, at £30 maximum, ranked above the average range of £10 to £20 for the 323 occupations listed in Campbell, *London Tradesman*, 331–40. Watch finishers could command up to £20 with an apprentice, and watch-movement-makers as much as £10, although chain-makers—a cottage industry dominated by women workers—had no apprentice fees. Lawyers charged £200 to take on a clerk, and positions with merchants and bankers cost even more. Among the lines of employment that did not necessitate an entrance fee, a few, such as physicians, required university training, but most were lesser skilled occupations—for example, hatband-makers and mop-makers. The distribution of apprenticeship fees for the 323 occupations are as follows: 27 percent cost £5 or less; 28 percent cost between £5 and £10; 28 percent cost between £10 and £20; and 17 percent cost more than £20.

46. George, *London Life*, 176; Baillie, Clutton, and Ilbert, *Britten's Old Clocks*, 270.

47. William Petty, "Another Essay in Political Arithmetick, Concerning the Growth of the City of London (1683)," in Charles Henry Hull, ed., *The Economic Writings of Sir William Petty*, 2 vols. (New York: Kelley, 1964), 2:473.

Mass production further encouraged changes in the retailing practices of watchmakers. Because timepieces were too fragile to be peddled in open stalls, their sale was moved indoors. Consequently, watchmakers were among the earliest artisans to establish their own shops to display their wares. Fully assembled watches arrayed in glass cases to safeguard them from weather tempted customers to select from a number of styles and to decide which additional decorations should be added to standard models. As chairs and other amenities appeared in the shops to make consumption more comfortable, workers frequently found themselves relegated to back rooms, separate workshops, or their own homes.[48]

By the time of William Moraley's apprenticeship, watchmaking had become highly specialized, generating the development of a number of auxiliary technical trades. Movement-makers, for example, supplied watch mechanisms, but they subcontracted various steps in the production process to cutters, pinion-makers, spring-makers, and chain-makers. Finishers assembled watches using additional parts from the cap- and stud-maker, watchcase-maker, dial-plate-maker, and hand- and key-maker. Independent workers, considered journeymen even though they themselves took on apprentices, commonly carried out each step of these operations. The watchmakers whose names appeared on the timepieces and who were the only people in the craft who could claim the status of master began to manufacture less and less of their own product. Instead, they operated increasingly as retailers, employers, and labor contractors.[49]

Mass production, a refined division of labor, and the deskilling of select work processes lowered the prices of watches and stimulated a vast expansion in the ownership of timepieces.[50] By the early eighteenth cen-

48. E. J. Tyler, *The Craft of the Clockmaker* (London: Ward, Lock, 1973), 24.

49. Ibid., 24–25, 62; David S. Landes, *Revolution in Time: Clocks and the Making of the Modern World* (Cambridge, Mass.: Belknap Press of Harvard University Press, 1983), 219–36. Even though the craft of clockmaking was minutely subdivided into various parts, it was still assumed that masters would know how to make all the moving components of a timepiece. In addition, many masters crafted tall clocks by custom order, with only the wooden case and perhaps the dial and its appurtenances contracted to other workers. Navigational and scientific instruments were also sometimes produced on individual customer order, and much of the innovative textile machinery of the eighteenth century is said to have been designed by watchmakers. Masters thus often remained skilled artisans even as their managerial and distributive functions increased. See George, *London Life*, 172–76; Campbell, *London Tradesman*, 250–53, 340; and Smith, *Wealth of Nations*, 129.

50. Adam Smith noted that watches in the mid-sixteenth century cost £20 but that the expense of a far more accurate timepiece was only £1 a century later (Smith, *Wealth of Nations*, 257). One result, as a

tury, masters like William Moraley Sr. could expect a handsome profit, while journeymen finishers earned considerably less, perhaps 30 or 40 shillings a week "if constantly employed." Journeymen workers in the lesser branches of the business averaged between one-quarter and one-half of the income of a finisher. Moreover, locating continual employment was often a problem, especially during downturns in England's economy. The country's financial contraction between 1728 and 1731 undoubtedly hampered Moraley's ability to find a job in London. Five percent of the debtors in London's Fleet Prison who applied for relief under the 1729 Insolvent Debtor's Act belonged to that craft.[51]

This was the highly specialized environment in which William Moraley first learned the art and mystery of watchmaking. It was, however, an environment unique to London. Clockmakers and watchmakers outside that metropolis, whether in rural areas or in large towns like Newcastle, sold watches, crafted tall clocks for individual clients, and kept their customers' timepieces clean, lubricated, and in repair, but could not compete with London's watchmaking industry. There were few clockmakers' companies outside the English capital and none in Newcastle, which meant that anyone might enter the trade, thereby increasing competition and lowering profits and wages.[52]

Moraley encountered the same problem faced by most journeymen who wanted to set themselves up as independent masters: the necessity of substantial capital. To rent a workshop and to purchase essential tools and raw materials for watchmaking and clockmaking cost between £50 and £100.[53] Obtaining a clientele, waiting for weeks or months for customers' payments, hiring journeymen, and taking on apprentices involved considerable additional expense. Benjamin Franklin's efforts to raise money for his own printing house are instructive about the plight of many journeymen. Franklin entered into a partnership with an alcoholic printer with few skills solely because his partner's father agreed to finance the business. Subsequently, Franklin borrowed from his friends and even bargained for a marriage, provided the dowry was sufficient to

visitor to London in 1719 observed, was that "everybody has a watch" (quoted in Roy Porter, *English Society in the Eighteenth Century* [London: Penguin, 1982], 301).

51. Campbell, *London Tradesman*, 252; George, *London Life*, 176; McCusker and Menard, *Economy of British America*, 62–64. Statistics about debtors in Fleet Prison were calculated from the *London Gazette*, nos. 6780–82, May 1729.

52. George, *London Life*, 176; Baillie, Clutton, and Ilbert, *Britten's Old Clocks*, 270–72.

53. Campbell, *London Tradesman*, 340; Baillie, Clutton, and Ilbert, *Britten's Old Clocks*, 267.

pay his debt and establish himself as a master.[54] The £300 Moraley expected from his father's will would have enabled him to become independent, but the £20 his mother gave him out of his father's estate was insufficient. It was his misfortune never to have either the constant employment or the lump sum from an inheritance that would have allowed him to establish himself as a prosperous master watchmaker.

In the colonies, the conditions of clockmakers and watchmakers were less organized and more primitive. Samuel Johnson observed about colonial manufacturing: "how many trades every man . . . is compelled to exercise, with how much labour the products of nature must be accommodated to human use, how long the loss or defect of any common utensil must be endured, or by what aukward expedients it must be supplied."[55] Colonial Burlington proved to be no exception to Johnson's dictum. Rural watchmakers in the colonies rarely specialized in a single craft. Moraley's owner, Isaac Pearson, was a master clockmaker who had apprenticed in Philadelphia, but he also worked as a silversmith, goldsmith, blacksmith, and buttonmaker. Pearson received additional income from his political and civic activities and from his investments in real estate and the iron forge at Mount Holly. The small, scattered population dotting the Delaware Valley owned relatively few timepieces during the early eighteenth century, and affluent residents frequently invested in land and labor rather than in consumer goods. An analysis of inventories of estates in southeastern Pennsylvania and northern Delaware between 1690 and 1735 found that only 5 percent of rural households and 25 percent of Philadelphia households owned a clock. This compares with clock ownership among 30 percent of English rural households and 50 percent of London households. Just 17 percent of the inventories listed any timepieces in Hunterdon and Burlington counties in New Jersey during the first half of the century, few of which were watches. Even in Philadelphia, "only men in easy circumstances carried a watch," and these often were London imports.[56] Moreover, a relatively

54. Lemisch, ed., *Benjamin Franklin*, 63–68, 80. Recognizing this serious problem for journeymen, Franklin provided £2,000 sterling in his will to be lent to young married artisans in Boston and Philadelphia, to enable them to set up their own shops (*Encouragement for Apprentices to be Sober . . .* , broadside, 1800, Historical Society of Pennsylvania; and Accounts Ledger, Franklin Legacy, 1791–1868, Philadelphia City Archives, City Hall Annex).

55. Samuel Johnson, "They Polish Life by Useful Arts (1753)," in Bertrand H. Bronson, ed., *Rasselas, Poems, and Selected Prose* (New York: Holt, Rinehart & Winston, 1958), 158.

56. See Jack Michel, "'In a Manner and Fashion Suitable to Their Degree': A Preliminary Investiga-

large number of clockmaker craftsmen lived in the Delaware Valley, meaning that competition was stiff and employment possibilities were limited.[57] Not for another generation would that region's clockmakers and watchmakers fashion a more fully developed industry along English lines.[58]

English-trained clockmakers must have been dismayed at the working conditions prevailing in the New World. Moraley not only repaired and

---

tion of the Material Culture of Early Rural Pennsylvania" (Paper presented to the Philadelphia Center for Early American Studies, 1981), 7, 75, 81; and Lorna Weatherill, *Consumer Behavior and Material Culture in Britain, 1660–1760* (London: Routledge, 1988), table 2.2, p. 27; and table 4.4, p. 89. See also Joan Jensen, *Loosening the Bonds: Mid-Atlantic Farm Women, 1750–1800* (New Haven: Yale University Press, 1986), 55. Information on New Jersey inventories, 1714–44 and 1759–89, is derived from samples collected by Judy A. McGaw as part of her continuing research project, which she generously shared with us before publication. Two-thirds of the timepieces inventoried in Burlington and Hunterton counties in the first half of the century were clocks; watches did not become common until the century's second half. Studies of inventories from rural Massachusetts and rural Maryland also found that very few households owned timepieces before mid-century. See Gloria L. Main, "The Standard of Living in Southern New England, 1640–1773," *William and Mary Quarterly*, 3rd ser., 45 (January 1988): 134; and Lois Green Carr and Lorena S. Walsh, "The Standard of Living in the Colonial Chesapeake," ibid., 146. Quotation from John F. Watson, *Annals of Philadelphia, and Pennsylvania, in the Olden Time*, 3 vols. (Philadelphia: Stuart, 1899), 1:218.

57. Moraley mentions four clockmakers in Philadelphia, two of whom quickly decided to try their luck elsewhere. He also indicates that he cleaned and repaired two timepieces in one day. If this were a normal workday, then four artisans, working the standard six-day week, could easily clean and repair 2,500 timepieces annually without the assistance of apprentices or journeymen. Yet the work of Jack Michel suggests that there were only about 350 clocks in the city, so it is doubtful that there was sufficient employment for four watchmakers and clockmakers in early Philadelphia. See Michel, "'In a Manner and Fashion Suitable to Their Degree'"; and Edward E. Chandlee, *Six Quaker Clockmakers* (Philadelphia: Historical Society of Pennsylvania, 1943). Pennsylvania was the center of the American trade, however, a factor that might have served to attract artisans. From the founding of the colonies until 1825, some 194 clockmakers are known to have worked in Pennsylvania, by far the largest number in any colony or state and more than one-fourth of all the clockmakers who operated in British North America. D. W. Hering, "Geographical Distribution of Early Clockmaking in America," *American Collector* 6, no. 10 (1937): 23. Still, Christopher Sauer presented a somewhat different view. In 1724 he wrote a letter from Philadelphia to Germany asserting that clockmakers could earn a good living in America (Donald F. Durnbaugh, "Christopher Sauer: Pennsylvania-German Printer," *PMHB* 83 [1958]: 324).

58. Finding sufficient manufacturing and repair work in the face of a saturated market remained a problem for watchmakers and clockmakers into the nineteenth century; see Philip Zea, "Clockmaking and Society at the River and the Bay: Jedidiah and Jabez Baldwin, 1790–1820," in Peter Benes, ed., *The Dublin Seminar for New England Folklife, Annual Proceedings, 1981: The Bay and the River, 1600–1900* (Boston: Boston University Press, 1982), 43–59. Nearly all studies of clockmaking in the eighteenth-century Delaware Valley focus on its technological aspects rather than on the economic development of the craft, but see Frank D. Prager, ed., *The Autobiography of John Fitch* (Philadelphia: American Philosophical Society, 1976); and Alfred Coxe Prime, *The Arts and Crafts in Philadelphia, Maryland, and South Carolina* (1929; reprint, New York: Da Capo Press, 1969), 1:225–73, 2:238–73.

cleaned timepieces, much as he would have done in northern England, but he had to tramp through the countryside to drum up business. In addition, he performed a variety of odd jobs unrelated to clockmaking. One result was that the clocks produced by Pearson's workshop (see Figure 14) generally were inferior to English standards of craftsmanship.[59] One of the still-extant clocks had "the appearance of English workmanship" and was "nicely proportioned and pleasing to the eye." Charles J. Burton points out, however, that the engraved inscription "TEMPUS FUGIT" (time flies) was misspelled "TEPUS FUG IT," with the missing "M" scratched in later above the "P." Moreover, the works of this clock employed wrought iron where brass should have been used; the plates were of varying thicknesses; and the copper was soft from being insufficiently worked.[60] The "aukward expedients" of colonial craftsmanship and the "many trades" undertaken with so much labor by Moraley and his fellow servants survive in the clocks bearing Pearson's name.

The difficulty of these conditions is evident in the reaction of four English clockmakers purchased by Moraley's master during the 1720s and 1730s. According to Moraley's account and Philadelphia newspaper advertisements (see Figure 17 and Appendix F), four servants absconded from Isaac Pearson, even though Moraley found him to be a "generous" master (82). The runaways shared similar characteristics. They were apparently recruited from provincial England rather than from London. Moraley came from Newcastle, another was "a West-Country Man, speaks by Clusters, hard to understand," and a 1723 clock from Pearson's shop was designed "as northern English makers generally preferred." The four men were nearly ten years older than typical servants, having spent their youth acquiring the skills of their trade. All were poorly dressed in inexpensive linen shirts and breeches and other old clothes. Two had shaved heads, indicating that they had been lousy, an affliction Moraley also endured. And most of them apparently at-

59. Seven clocks from the workshop of Isaac Pearson have survived (see Figure 14). Only one is dated, and none indicates the names of journeymen or apprentices. The seven clocks are described in the Decorative Arts Catalogue located in the Winterthur Museum. We thank Bert Denker, curator of the catalogue, for his generous assistance.

60. Charles J. Burton, "A New Jersey Clock," *Bulletin of the National Association of Watch and Clock Collectors* 8 (1958): 213–14. The clock is tentatively dated to 1735, about the time of Moraley's indenture. See also Carl M. Williams, *Silversmiths of New Jersey, 1700–1825, with Some Notice of Clockmakers who Were Also Silversmiths* (Philadelphia: George S. McManus, 1949), 34–44; and Elaine Brenchley, "Isaac Pearson: Clockmaker of Burlington, West Jersey" (Apprentice Guide Paper, Winterthur Museum Library, 1982).

tempted to gain their freedom early in their term, since Pearson could not remember the name of one servant and was unsure about the age of another.[61]

As a clockmaker, Moraley stood relatively little chance of prospering in the Delaware Valley, a fact recognized by the London recruiter who informed him frankly that his trade was "of little Service to the *Americans*" (52) and who thereby extracted an extra year's service from him. Moreover, Moraley was the last of his nineteen shipmates to be sold, and Pearson purchased him for the bargain price of £11 for a five-year stint, compared with the average £12 cost for four years of service for most servants in Pennsylvania.[62] Once free, Moraley not only earned modest wages in a Philadelphia watchmaker's shop—less than a third of what London journeymen earned—but also was unable to secure regular employment. He tried to support himself by tramping door-to-door repairing and cleaning timepieces, but found too little work. When he became a tinker as well, a skill foreign to him, he failed.[63] Moraley finally resorted to blacksmithing, which he had learned as Pearson's servant. The work was more physically demanding and paid only 8 shillings a week, but at least it promised steady employment. The 1730s were not propitious times for watchmakers who had no capital or connections in the Delaware Valley. It was another of Moraley's misfortunes to have arrived in the region forty years before the local economy was able to support additional artisans in that trade. He wisely decided to return to England to renew his struggle for a share of his mother's estate.

But his return was not crowned with success. After the death of his mother, Moraley again failed to secure the lump sum of money he desired. His debts and attempts to break the elaborate provisions of his

61. Moraley was 31 years old when he fled, while the others were 26, 30, and 37. See William Nelson, ed., *Documents Relating to the Colonial History of the State of New Jersey*, vol. 11: *Extracts from American Newspapers, Relating to New Jersey, 1:1704–1739* (Paterson, N.J.: The Press Printing and Publishing Co., 1894), quotations from 124, 301–2, 510. On the style of clocks, see "An Analysis of the Isaac Pearson Tall Clock in the Vauxhall Room, Winterthur" (Typescript, 1986, deposited at the Burlington County Historical Society), quotation on 19.

62. According to Farley Grubb, in 1746 in Philadelphia 432 male indentured servants sold for an average of 15.5 Pennsylvania pounds for an average of 4.44 years of servitude, or £3.49 a year ("Market for Indentured Immigrants," 858). Salinger calculated that in 1745 one year of an indentured servant's time in Pennsylvania cost approximately £3.06 (*"To Serve Well and Faithfully,"* 143).

63. Many itinerant clock repairers practiced the tinker's trade in addition to their own, even in the nineteenth century. Richardson Wright, *Hawkers and Walkers in Early America* (1927; reprint, New York: Frederick Ungar, 1965), 58.

mother's will cost him most of the remaining estate, and in the end he was no better capitalized than before. Worse, he now had no hope of a windfall inheritance. All he could manage thereafter was, as John Wilson later recalled, to settle in Newcastle, where he "contrived to make a livelihood as a Watchmaker" for the last two decades of his life.[64]

The Social, Political, and Religious Worlds of William Moraley

William Moraley's employment imposed on him a status of dependency throughout most of his life. As a clerk, apprentice, indentured servant, journeyman, and ship's cook, Moraley was expected to follow orders and to serve his masters and employers. Indeed, clerks, apprentices, and servants "belonged" to their masters, and their rights were severely curtailed by law and custom. Like other bound workers, Moraley could neither marry nor participate in the political process.

In early eighteenth-century England, youths customarily spent their adolescence and early adulthood as either servants or apprentices. Marriage was discouraged until they gained their freedom, accumulated necessary household goods, learned the basic skills of their trade, and achieved the ability to support a family. For most English citizens these requirements meant late marriages; on average, women wed at age twenty-six, and men wed at twenty-eight. Relatively rare, and much criticized, were people who undertook familial responsibilities before realizing economic and social independence. Celibacy and dependency characterized the normal and expected condition of young men and women, and of at least one out of every nine of Moraley's adult peers who never became sufficiently autonomous to marry.[65]

Moraley led a single life in a largely male world. His account, like many adventure tales, is part of the liturgy of masculinism in which men relate to one another while women play but minor roles. Moraley's

64. Manuscript sheet tipped into the University of Michigan William L. Clements Library copy of Moraley's autobiography and attributed to Thomas Bell. See Appendix A.

65. John R. Gillis, *For Better, For Worse: British Marriages, 1600 to the Present* (New York: Oxford University Press, 1985), esp. 161–65; E. A. Wrigley and R. S. Schofield, *The Population History of England, 1541–1871: A Reconstruction* (Cambridge: Cambridge University Press, 1989), 255–60.

interactions with women were limited, especially while he was indentured. Among the servants who emigrated from England to Pennsylvania between 1729 and 1734, men outnumbered women by eleven to one.[66] It is not surprising that Moraley's recruiter sent him off with a wish for "a prosperous Voyage and a good Wife" (53), and Moraley found that none of his fellow servants on board the *Boneta* was a woman. Prosperity and marriage were intimately linked but difficult to obtain for propertyless former male servants.[67] Because of the gender imbalance among bound workers, the colonies receiving large numbers of immigrants were often disproportionately male.[68] Moraley worked, drank, and conversed primarily with other men.[69] His enforced unmarried state even caused him briefly to envy slaves who wed and had children, he thought, because "the Negro need fear no Expense" (95) in rearing his offspring. Slaves, that is, were spared the requirement of economic independence when establishing their families. It was not accidental that Moraley believed himself "oppressed by Dame Fortune" (50) because both fortune (in part because of his mother) and a wife eluded him. As long as he was the property of his master Moraley could not claim a spouse as his own possession.[70]

Moraley viewed most women as a type of property. In assessing the status of an English parson, he noted that "the best of his Goods" was "a handsome brown Wife" (136). He courted an "old ugly Maid" to gain

66. Calculated from Galenson, *White Servitude*, 219–37.

67. Moraley observes that only proffered marriage to handsome women with good fortunes induced some men to stay in Pennsylvania.

68. According to the census of 1737–38, there were 122 men over the age of sixteen for every 100 women in Burlington County, New Jersey; this was one of the most unbalanced sex ratios in the colony (Peter O. Wacker, *Land and People: A Cultural Geography of Preindustrial New Jersey: Origins and Settlement Patterns* [New Brunswick, N.J.: Rutgers University Press, 1975], 146). Among Philadelphia Anglicans between 1729 and 1734, burials of males outnumbered burials of females by 136 to 100. Calculated from Mr. Archibald Cummings's Private Register, Christ Church (GSP).

69. Another down-and-out Philadelphia watchmaker also was celibate for long periods. John Fitch wrote: "I Sir for Twenty-two years have never sought after woman but rather chose to avoid them and have in that time frequantly treated the sex unbecoming a man. For which I ask their Pardon. I have in this time kept a solemn Lent for more than seven years together" (Prager, *Autobiography of John Fitch*, 137). Franklin was much less disciplined in this matter. His "hard-to-be-governed passion of youth had hurried me frequently into intrigues with low women that fell in my way" (Lemisch, ed., *Benjamin Franklin*, 81).

70. It is not known whether Moraley ever wed. A number of marriages that list the groom as William Morley/Morrowley/Moraley were recorded in Northumberland and Durham counties during the period between Moraley's return to Newcastle and his death in 1762. The records are incomplete, and none of the surviving accounts can be definitely linked to the author.

"possession of her Moveables" (110). He observed that men sometimes were enticed to remain in the colonies because of the "handsome" women, many of whom "have good Fortunes" (104). These calculations about women could become the basis for male bonding. Moraley engaged in a "merry Discourse" with his patron, Mr. Senhouse, about "which of his Maids I liked the best" (136), although Moraley wisely refrained from actually claiming one of the servants. And indeed, not only were eighteenth-century women subsumed under the identities of their fathers, husbands, and guardians, but wives also enriched their spouses with their household goods, with their labor, and in many cases with a dowry or inheritance. All this became, by law, the property of their husband at marriage.

Yet Moraley did not perceive every woman in such a calculated fashion. He treated women who were his social superiors equally with men of similar status. He fought with his mother and authorized his lawyer to threaten her with legal penalties, just as he twice brought his male masters to court. He dealt with mother and master in an analogous, hardheaded manner when he felt that agreements had been unilaterally abrogated, although he reverted to a dependent position with both once the dispute was resolved. In another context the Lambert family members became his patrons after he rescued Hannah Lambert from drowning. Hannah's father, Thomas, adopted Moraley as a retainer, providing him with money and lodging, and after Thomas's death Hannah dispensed similar favors to a suitably humble Moraley. When he met Sarah Pearson, his master's unmarried daughter, Moraley refrained from coldly assessing the value of her property and instead became "enamour'd" of her (77). Both rank and gender were important determinants of Moraley's behavior and attitudes.

Moraley's lack of material success meant that he did not qualify to vote. Yet he held strong political beliefs, as clearly expressed in his reworking of George Webb's poem. While peace, judicial rights, and constitutional monarchy were components of the ideal state in both the original and the revised versions, Moraley substituted "laws and liberties" (66) for "life and property" (159) as the most important rights guaranteed to all British subjects. This alteration reflects the interest of the poorer sort in restraining the powerful and the privileged. Moraley likewise recognized the gulf between the unfortunates and the fortunates in society. While accepting charity, he observed that "Men in plentiful Circumstances, seldom or never consider the Wants of the Needy"

(136). He abhorred aristocratic prerogative, contrasting the affluence of freeholders of the Delaware Valley to conditions in "England, where Gentlemen live on the Labour of the Farmer" (87) and where all inhabitants found "Lords of Manors to hamper them with their Privileges" (101). He also commented favorably on communal ideals, noting that fruit in Pennsylvania is "common to the weary Traveller, as well as the wealthy Citizen, it being no Trespass to gather them" (68) and that "Hunting is allowed" (101) on private property to all people. Moraley felt justified in having "made free" (53) with the ship captain's private supply of raisins. Still, Moraley's solution to his own unfortunate situation was not to advocate enfranchising the "lowest Class of Men" (104) but to rise in rank by inheriting his parents' estate.

Although neither a master, nor a head of a family, nor a voter, Moraley was a staunch member of the Church of England. Like many contemporary artisans, scientists, and intellectuals, he found the physical world to be a sacred testament to the existence of a "Beneficent Creator," filled with "infinite Wisdom," "Goodness, Power and Mercy" (92). As a clockmaker, Moraley was naturally curious about the efficiencies of machines and how they worked. His memoirs are filled with observations about the wonders of nature and the order of the universe, all of which cause him to admire the "Effects of the Divine Providence in supporting the most minute of his Productions" (93).

Moraley's God demanded that His followers practice forgiveness and charity to all, aside from the one uneasy exception of slavery, where "Necessity" (93) justified barbarities that go against the principles of Christianity and the values of the British people. Belief and morality would be rewarded by salvation in the hereafter, not by material gain in this life. This God did not empower Moraley; his prayers of thanksgiving were offered only for favors already bestowed. Even his conversion-like experience was not addressed to God. Moraley understood his vow to "reform my Life and Conversation" and to turn from "sinful Thought" as "ruminating with myself," and his hoped-for reward would flow from "good Fortune" (113) rather than from divine intervention.

God did intervene in Moraley's world to instruct, if not to reward. The natural world instilled "moral Precepts" (101) even in heathens, and Moraley found religious inspiration and proof of divine providence in his observation of New World plants and animals. Ghosts too were sent by God for moral instruction. Moraley's ejaculation on seeing the ghost of a murdered slave, "Lord! why do you come here?" (83), was an expression of awe rather than a profane oath.[71] Evil had no objective existence for Moraley. Since Satan did not exist, he could scoff at people who believed in witches, yet simultaneously entertain a superstitious belief in ghosts. Moraley shared the latitudinarian faith of many educated English people of his time. He admired the Quakers and briefly passed himself off as a Roman Catholic, but still assumed that, if given the chance, most reasonable humans would embrace the Anglican faith.

While his distant and somewhat impersonal God allowed Moraley freedom to exercise his own will, this also left him vulnerable to forces beyond his control. In Moraley's cosmos, secular advantage and disadvantage often were attributed to the amoral, unpredictable, and uncontrollable power of fate, luck, chance, and fortune. Life made continual sport of humans, their reason, their hopes, and their ambitions. Moraley frequently invoked the random forces of misfortune rather than his own individual responsibility to explain his lack of success. He concluded his account of his adventures as "a living Monument of God's Mercy" (143), but it was an unhappy memorial resigned to the meanest employ, necessity, hardship, and affliction.

71. Joseph Addison argued in 1711 that ghosts were the agents of divine morality. They were "almost certain proof of the immortality of the soul," and those who heeded their warnings "are excited to the study of virtue" (Mary E. Litchfield, ed., *The Roger de Coverley Papers from the Spectator* [Boston: Athenaeum, 1902], 44).

THE INFORTUNATE:

OR, THE

VOYAGE and ADVENTURES

OF

WILLIAM MORALEY,

Of MORALEY, in the County of *Northumberland*, Gent.

From his BIRTH, to the PRESENT TIME.

CONTAINING,

Whatever is curious and remarkable in the Provinces of *Pensilvania* and *New Jersey*; an Account of the Laws and Customs of the Inhabitants; the Product, Soil and Climate; also the AUTHOR's several Adventures through divers Parts of *America*, and his surprising Return to *Newcastle*.

To which is added,

His CASE, recommended to the Gentlemen of the Law.

Written by HIMSELF.

Fœlix quem faciunt aliena pericula cautum. HOR.

——— *Si quid novisti rectius istis,*
Candidus imperti; si non, his utere mecum. HOR.

NEWCASTLE:
Printed by J. WHITE, for the AUTHOR; and sold by the Booksellers in Town and Country.

MDCCXLIII.

[EDITORS' NOTE: The title page of *The Infortunate*, reproduced on the other side of this page, was photographed by the William L. Clements Library, University of Michigan, and is used by permission. The word "infortunate" (rather than "unfortunate") was more commonly used in Shakespeare's time than later, during the eighteenth century. Moraley reserves "infortunate" for the title and uses the modern spelling in the body of his memoirs. It is possible that Moraley's choice of the word is based on the play *The Banish'd Duke; or, The Tragedy of Infortunatus* (London: Baldwin, 1690), a thinly disguised, anonymous account of the Duke of Monmouth's ill-fated attempt to overthrow James II in 1685. Like Moraley, Infortunatus is banished by his family. He bewails his fate in exile: "Whilst all my Forces (plainly to confess) / Are raw, unarm'd, and I am moneyless. / From sorrow's Scene I do contemplate now / What base deceitful peoples brought me to." And Moraley would have agreed with Infortunatus's politics and fatalism: "Since time began, ne're was a juster cause; / Than Lives, Religion, Liberty and Laws; / We fight for Heaven, our Kingdom, Church and State, / Submitting all we have to Divine Fate." (Quotations from pp. 20 and 28.)

The first epigraph on the title page, attributed to Horace, means "Happy is he who is warned by another's danger." It does not, however, come from Horace (see Dominicus Bo., *Lexicon Horatianum*, 2 vols. [Hildensheim: Georg Olms, 1965]). Benjamin Franklin used it as the heading for the following comic piece in *Poor Richard's Almanack for 1734*:

> *Felix quem faciunt aliena pericula cautum.*
> To such a height th' Expence of COURTS is gone,
> That poor Men are redress'd—*till they're undone.*

> *William, your Cause is good, give me my Fee, and I'll defend it.* But, alas! William is cast, the Verdict goes against him. *Give me another Fee, and I'll move the Court in Arrest of Judgment.* Then Sentence is confirmed. *T'other Fee, and I'll bring a Writ of Error.* But judgment is again confirm'd, and *Will* condemn'd to pay Costs. What shall we do now, Master, says William. *Why since it can't be helpt, there's no more to be said; pay the Knave his Money, and I'm satisfied.*

> Of disposition they're most sweet,
> Their clients always kindly greet;
> And tho' at Bar they rip old Sores,
> And brawl and scold like drunken Wh——s,
> Their Angers in a moment pass
> Away at Night over a Glass;
> Nay often laugh at the Occasion
> Of their premeditated Passion.
> *O may you prosper as you treat us,*
> *Until the* D——l *sign your* Quietus.

Franklin borrowed his foreign language aphorisms from James Howell's *Lexicon Tetraglotton* of 1660. See Van Wyck Brooks, ed., *Poor Richard: The Almanacks for the Years 1733–1758* (New York: Ballantine, 1976), 23–24, 295.

The second epigraph is indeed from Horace (*Epistles*, 1.6.68: "To Numicus"). A contemporary translation of both lines is: "[Live and be happy.] If you know any maxims better than these, impart them with your usual candor; if not, make the best use you can of mine" (David Watson, *The Works of Horace Translated into English Prose*, 2 vols. [1739; reprint, New York: AMS, 1976], 2:232). This epigraph was commonly employed in eighteenth-century literature. Pope, Addison, Steele, Fielding, and Chesterfield used these lines in publications that appeared during Moraley's lifetime. See Caroline Grad, *Horace in the English Literature of the Eighteenth Century* (New Haven: Yale University Press, 1916).]

THE PREFACE

MY Design in prefixing this *Preface*, is to return the Worthy Gentlemen of *Newcastle*,[1] and Parts adjacent, my most sincere and hearty Thanks for the many Favours they have bestow'd on me, undeservedly. At present, I have no other Way to retaliate them; therefore hope they will accept of these my weak Endeavours, as a Specimen of my Gratitude.

There are in the following Pages many Observations to be found, which are not to be met with, perhaps, in other Authors; I having an Opportunity, the Time I was abroad, of conversing with the most substantial Planters, from whom I was inform'd of many Particulars relating to the Laws and Customs of the Provinces I resided in.

On the Whole, I have advanc'd nothing but what I know to be Truth, in however rough and homely a Dress it may happen to appear;

1. See Appendix E for more information about Newcastle.

and compos'd it, not only to reflect on the unhappy State of Life l was reduced to by my Inconsideration, but to persuade Mankind, that the only Way to avoid the like Difficulties, is to take care how they misapply their Talents, and endeavour to improve 'em to a better Purpose than the most unfortunate of Mankind.

W. MORALEY.

1 MORALEY AND HIS FAMILY—THE INFORTUNATE LEARNS LATIN AND ARITHMETIC—BOUND TO AN ATTORNEY—BECOMES A WATCHMAKER—THE SOUTH SEA BUBBLE—HIS MOTHER SETTLES IN NEWCASTLE—REDUCED TO POVERTY—SELLS HIMSELF FOR A TERM OF YEARS INTO THE AMERICAN PLANTATIONS—BEFORE THE LORD MAYOR OF LONDON—REPENTING TOO LATE—CALLING AT CALAIS—A RECOGNITION.

THE Calamities that afflict human Nature are generally owing to the imprudent Management of their Affairs. A sad Instance of the Truth of this Reflection, the following Relation contains, which is communicated to the World, in order to induce Mankind to act with Caution and Discretion, that they may avoid the Inconveniences and Disappointments which attend the Unwary and Inconsiderate.

London is the Place of my Nativity, which was in the Year 1698. My Parents were of no mean Account, and in good Circumstances, my Father being the third and youngest Son of a Gentleman, Chief of an ancient Family and considerable Estate, descended from the Barons *Morley*, of *Swanton Morley*, in *Norfolk*. By Charter from King *Edward* I.[1] he held Lands in *Northumberland*, bearing his Name, which were increased by Purchase; and in the last Century were augmented by two Marriages, first by *William Moraley*, my Great Great Grandfather, with *Elizabeth*,

1. Edward I reigned from 1272 to 1307.

Daughter to *Nicolas Ridley*, of *Willemoteswick*, in *Com. Northumb'*, Esq; and secondly, by *Agnes*, Daughter of *Alexander Ridley*, of *Whitsheals*, third Brother of the said *Nicolas Ridley*, to *Thomas Moraley*, Son of the above *William Moraley*.

By this Alliance, large Possessions were added to the Paternal Estate; which passing from the Family by the Extravagance of my Father's elder Brother, he was oblig'd to seek his Fortune, and became a Citizen of *London*, where he married *Martha*, the Daughter of Mr *John Mason*, a wealthy Founder and Citizen.[2] Her Mother, nam'd *Martha*, was Daughter of *Henry Stevens*, of *Steventon*, in *Com. Berks*,[3] Esq; allied to the Family of *Sonds*, of *Lees Court*, in *Com. Cantii*,[4] in the Person of Sir *George Sonds*, Knight of the Bath, afterwards created Earl of *Faversham* by King *Charles* II.[5] whose eldest Daughter was married to *Lewis*, Marquis of *Blanquefort*, Baron *Duras* in *England*, who, by the Death of Sir *George*, became, by Reversion, Earl of *Faversham*, in right of his Wife. He was second Brother to *Charles d'Urfort de Duras*, Duke and Marshal of *France*. The second Daughter of Sir *George* married Sir *Lewis Watson*, afterwards Lord *Rockingham*, Grandfather to the present Earl of *Rockingham*.

I mention this not out of Ostentation, but because some People have represented her as meanly descended: For my part, I do not think true Honour consists in an Alliance to a Coronet; but, on the contrary, they

2. Moraley's father served three masters in quick succession, finally spending seven years with Thomas Tompion as an apprentice. Moraley achieved his freedom in 1688 and afterward was hired by Tompion as a journeyman worker. The Office of the Archbishop of Canterbury in Knightrider Street, London, issued the marriage license for Moraley's parents on November 24, 1697. The apprenticeship of Moraley's father appears in Charles Edward Atkins, *Register of Apprentices of the Worshipful Company of Clockmakers of the City of London from Its Incorporation in 1631 to Its Tercentenary in 1931* (Privately printed, 1931), 203. Moraley's father gave a brief summary of his career when advertising his move from London to Newcastle-upon-Tyne: "William Moraley, Clock and Watch-Maker, who served his Time with, and wrought for the famous Mr. Tompion at London, till his Decease [November 20, 1713], is lately come into his Native Country, and designs to reside in Newcastle upon Tine, who makes and sells Gold and Silver-Watches, mends and cleans all Sorts of Clocks or Watches; and is to be met with at John Morley's House, next Door to the Black and the Grey, in the Big-Market, Newcastle" (*Newcastle Weekly Courant*, August 24, 1723, 10–11). The date of the marriage license of Moraley's parents is in George E. Cokayne and Edward Alexander Fry, eds., *The Index Library: Calendar of Marriage Licenses Issued by the Faculty Office, 1632–1714* (London: By subscription, 1905), 153. William Moraley's birth is recorded in Willoughby A. Littledale, ed., *The Registers of Christ Church, Newgate, 1538 to 1754*, Publications of the Harleian Society—Registers (London: Harleian Society, 1895), 21, 91.

3. Berkshire.

4. Cambridgeshire.

5. Charles II reigned from 1680 to 1685.

Figure 1. *"Industry and Idleness*, 1: 'The Fellow 'Prentices at their Looms'" (William Hogarth, 1747). The two apprentices start their careers in identical circumstances, but one is industrious and the other is idle.

that behave themselves in the most virtuous and humble Manner, deserve the greatest Esteem.

In my Infancy, such care was taken of me, by an Education suitable to their Circumstances, as laid the Foundation of all the Evils that have since befallen me, by the over Indulgence of my Parents. In a more advanced Age, I was taught the *Latin* Tongue, with Arithmetick, besides Musick and Dancing. I had likewise an Opportunity of conversing with the *Royal Society*,[6] and by that Means have gone through several Courses of *Natural Philosophy*, by which I might have preferr'd myself; but being of too lively a Disposition, I neglected to improve my Talents, always preferring the present Time to the future; so that all these Advantages were bestow'd on me to no Purpose.

6. The Royal Society of London for Improving Natural Knowledge, founded in 1645.

Figure 2. *"Industry and Idleness*, 6: 'The Industrious 'Prentice out of his Time, & Married to his Master's Daughter'" (William Hogarth, 1747). The industrious apprentice advances in his profession by marrying the master's daughter.

At 15 Years of Age, my Father bound me Clerk to an eminent Attorney in the Lord Mayor's Court,[7] where I continued near two Years; but my Father not liking the Profession of the Law, by reason of the many Quirks[8] and Shifts[9] used by the Gentlemen Practitioners, with the Advice of *Henry May*, Esq; Recorder of the City of *Chichester*, formerly a

7. Exercising both judicial and administrative functions, the Lord Mayor's Court was one of the most important in the country. It consisted of the mayor, aldermen, and a recorder and met in the King's Bench, Guildhall. See Walter Besant, *London in the Eighteenth Century* (London: Black, 1903), 201.

8. Subtleties, artful distinctions. E. L. McAdam Jr. and George Milne, eds., *Johnson's Dictionary: A Modern Selection* (New York: Pantheon, 1963), 327. All definitions are from this source unless otherwise noted.

9. Expedients found or used with difficulty.

Figure 3. *"Industry and Idleness*, 10: 'The Industrious 'Prentice, Alderman of London, the Idle one brought before him & Impeach'd by his Accomplice'" (William Hogarth, 1747). The two apprentices meet again when the idle one is apprehended for murder and brought to judgment before the industrious one, now Alderman of London.

Spanish Merchant, join'd to that of *William Carr*, Esq;[10] a Commissioner of the Excise, and Member of Parliament for *Newcastle*, took me from my Employ, and learnt me the Trade of Watch-making.

In my Clerkship, I did little else but vapour[11] about the Streets, with my Sword by my Side; as for studying the Law, little of that serv'd me, my Time being taken up with pursuing the Pleasures of the Town: Company was the Thing I chiefly thought on, and how to support it; which my Father perceiving, being an austere Man, closely observ'd my

10. William Carr (d. 1742) was elected to Parliament from Newcastle as a Whig for the years 1722–27 and 1729–34. He also served as mayor of the city in 1724 and 1737. See Romney Sedgwick, *The House of Commons, 1715–1754*, 2 vols. (New York: Oxford, 1970), 1:532.

11. To bully or brag.

Figure 4. "An Emblematical Print on the South Sea Scheme" (William Hogarth, 1721). This engraving is an allegory of the rampant speculation in the South Sea Company, which failed in 1720. The work depicts investors consumed by a speculative frenzy at the expense of middle-class values of industry and frugality. A merry-go-round operated by the South Sea Company stands in the center. The guild hall (where Moraley's apprenticeship was changed from attorney to watchmaker) stands on the left. Having taken possession of Fortune, a devil butchers her and throws her flesh to the crowd.

Actions, and mildly told me the Inconveniencies that would arise, if I did not take up in time, and reform, such as Loss of Friends, and a general Contempt from Mankind. He calmly told me, if I would follow his Directions, he would give me all the Encouragement that lay in his Power, by advancing my Fortune when a proper Time offer'd; and added, that *Virtue carries along with it its own Reward.*[12] My coming home had this good Effect, that it took me from my former loose Companions, the Bane of Youth; and after this, I became tractable, and obedient to my Father's Commands.

12. William Moraley, the author, was apprenticed to his father on May 5, 1718, for an unspecified number of years; apparently he never completed his apprenticeship. See Atkins, *Register of Apprentices*, 204.

Figure 5. Interior of a clockmaker's shop (Thomas Rowlandson, 1783). This provincial English store contains large display windows, a glass case full of assembled watches, and a comfortable chair for customers.

About this time, the World run mad after the *South Sea* Bubble.[13] My Father was bit to the Tune of £800, which somewhat impair'd his Fortune; and being advanc'd in Years, proposed to my Mother to settle at *Newcastle*, where he had many Friends. She declin'd this Proposal for some Years, but at last agreed to it, by my giving her a good Account of the Place, where I had been some Years before.

We arriv'd at *Newcastle* after two Days Sail, and settled for about two Years, meeting with Encouragement in our Business from the generous Inhabitants. In the meantime, my Father having Notice of the Death of his Brother, left us, in order to secure his Effects, but unfortunately died at *Harwich*, in his Passage home from *London*, in the Year 1725, from which Time I date all my Misfortunes. He had made a Will, which not answering my Expectations, occasioned frequent Quarrels and Contests between my Mother and myself; and her marrying again,[14] widen'd the Breach, and oblig'd me to leave *Newcastle* for *London*, where I arrived with 12 s[hillings] only, given me by my Mother, to *seek my Fortune*, she assuring me she could not raise any more, by reason of her Marriage.[15]

The Money being soon spent, and not readily falling into Business, I was reduc'd to Poverty. A Gentleman[16] let her know my Circumstances. She answer'd, she had given all out of her Power, and could do no more for me. He writ to her again, threatening her, if she did not restore the

13. Many Englishmen speculated wildly in the South Sea Company during the second decade of the eighteenth century. Although the company enjoyed a monopoly of trade in the South Seas, it was primarily a financial enterprise designed to assume the national debt and to use its credit to finance capital expansion. But the South Sea Company's directors, seeking to get rich quick, employed various shady means to inflate stock prices and realize large capital gains. The crash of 1720 ended the speculative frenzy, depleted the fortunes of many investors, and shook the government to its foundations. (Figure 4 is William Hogarth's engraving depicting the catastrophe of the South Sea Bubble.) See John Carswell, *The South Sea Bubble* (Stanford, Calif.: Stanford University Press, 1960); and J. H. Plumb, *The First Four Georges: England and Her "German" Kings, 1714–1830* (Boston: Little, Brown & Co., 1956), 62–64.

14. Martha Moralee married Charles Isaacson on October 19, 1728, at St. Andrew's Church in Newcastle. Isaacson, the son of Anthony and Jane Isaacson, was fifty-three years old, having been baptized in 1675 both at St. Nicholas Church in Newcastle and at a nonconformist church. (IGI.)

15. Married women did not exercise control over their property after their wedding unless a prenuptial agreement placed it in trust. Blackstone later summarized British law on the relations between husband and wife: "By marriage, the husband and wife are one person in law: that is, the very being or legal existence of the woman is suspended during the marriage. . . . [She] is therefore called in our law-French, a femme covert, and is said to be under the protection and influence of her husband, her baron, or lord; and her condition during her marriage is called her coverture" (J. W. Ehrlich, *Ehrlich's Blackstone, Part One: Rights of Persons, Rights of Things* [New York: Capricorn, 1959], 83).

16. Moraley's lawyer.

Figure 6. The Second Royal Exchange. Moraley went here to find information about a passage to America.

third Part of the Personal Effects to me, he would do me Justice; and withal let her know, he had applied to the Chamber of *London* on my Account. She answer'd him, if he or I gave her Trouble, she would leave all she had a Right to, from me: So the Affair dropp'd. I had now my Ingenuity to trust to; and it was in vain to expect any Subsistence from her.

The said Gentleman writ another Letter to her, and told her, it was needless to contend with me, for I was resolv'd to have my Right, notwithstanding my Father's Will, and any Release I could give her, unless she could prove I receiv'd my whole Fortune from her, a Release only standing good for so much as I had receiv'd, which was but £20 for the Acquittance of about £300 (for the Lord Mayor's Court being a Court of Equity, Remedy would be had against such an Imposition) and advised her to restore me the remainder.

But not hearing from her, I being resolute, as not caring what became of me, it enter'd into my Head to leave *England*, and sell myself for a Term of Years into the *American* Plantations. Accordingly I repair'd to the *Royal Exchange*, to inform myself, by the printed Advertisements fix'd against the Walls, of the Ships bound to *America*; where musing by myself, a Man[17] accosted me in the following Manner. Sir, said he, I have for some time observ'd you, and fancy your Condition of Life is alter'd for the worse, and guess you have been in better Circumstances; but if you will take my Advice, I'll make it my Business to find out some way which may be of Service to you. Perhaps you may imagine I have a Design to inveigle you, but I assure you I have none; and if you will accept of a Mug of Beer, I will impart what I have to propose to you. The Man appearing sincere, I gave Ear to him.

I was dress'd at that Time in a very odd Manner. I had on a Red Rug[18] Coat, with Black Lining, Black Buttons and Button Holes, and Black Lace upon the Pockets and Facing; an old worn out Tye Wig, which had not been comb'd out for above a Fortnight; an unshaven Beard; a torn Shirt, that had not been wash'd for above a Month; bad Shoes; and Stockings all full of Holes.

After he had shav'd me, he proposed to me an *American* Voyage, and said there was a Ship at *Limehouse* Dock, that would sail for *Pensilvania* in three or four Days. Sir, said I, a Person like me, oppress'd by Dame Fortune, need not care where he goes. All Places are alike to me; and I am very willing to accept of your Offer, if I could have some View of bettering my Condition of Life, though I might have expected a better Fate than to be forc'd to leave my Native Country: But adverse Fortune

17. According to the servitude contract for "William Morley" recorded on October 13, 1729, the man was Neal MacNeal. Moraley's destination is given as the Caribbean island of Antigua, but this merely indicates that MacNeal sent the bulk of his recruits to that destination. Historian John Wareing explains: "After 1724 it appears to have been the practice of the clerks who made up the register to take a bundle of indenture forms drawn up by an agent during a particular month and to enter the destination from just one of them as the destination for the whole group, even when a variety of destinations were involved." MacNeal did file Moraley's indenture along with a number of others. Moraley's name was spelled "Morley" on the contract, but, as Wareing and numerous other historians have noted, there was no standard spelling of surnames in the eighteenth century. The family itself used or tolerated variant spellings, including Moraley, Moreley, Morley, Morrowley, Moralee, and Morralee. The name is spelled both as Moraley and as Morley in the two surviving signatures of Moraley's mother. His father's will contains three different variants of the surname. Still, it is possible that the extant indenture contract is not the one signed by the author of these memoirs. See John Wareing, *Emigrants to America: Indentured Servants Recruited in London, 1718–1733* (Baltimore: Genealogical Publishing Co., 1985); quotations on 8–9, 77.

18. A coarse woolen cloth.

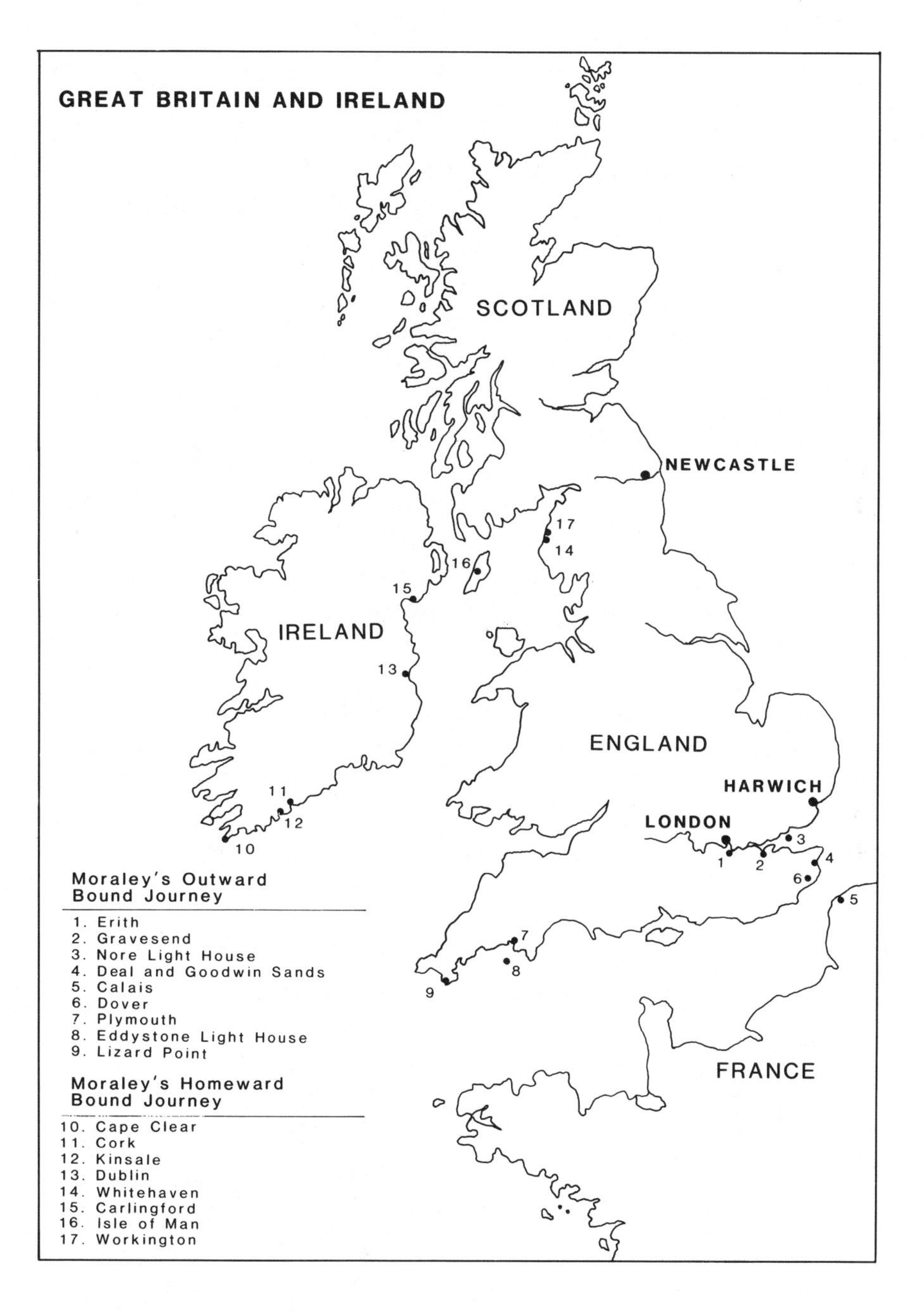

Map 1. Great Britain and Ireland.

is become familiar to me, by a Series of Misfortunes; so had rather leave a Place where I have no Prospect of advancing myself, than to continue here where I have no Friends to relieve me. Besides, in a distant Place, not being known, no Person can reflect on me for any ill Management, which oftentimes discourages one's Friends from supporting one, knowing the ill Use that is made of their Support.

Sir, says the Person, I'm entirely of your Way of Thinking, and believe you will better yourself by following my Advice. I will recommend you to the Captain, who is bound for *Philadelphia*, in *Pennsilvania*, a Country producing everything necessary for the Support of Life; and when your Time is expir'd, you will be free to live in any of the Provinces of *America*.

Then he ask'd me, if I was bred to any Business. I told him, Watchmaking was my Occupation. He said, he was afraid I would not do for any other Business, that being of little Service to the *Americans*; the useful Trades being, Bricklayers, Shoemakers, Barbers, Carpenters, Joiners, Smiths, Weavers, Bakers, Tanners, and Husbandmen more useful than all the rest.[19] They bind themselves for four Years; but if I would consent to bind myself for five, he said he would undertake to get me admitted. Those Men Brokers have generally for their Pains Three Half Crowns,[20] given them by the Masters of those Vessels which they are employ'd for.

After we had drank two Pints of Beer, he paid the Reckning. I absolutely agreed to go, and to that Intent we went before Sir *Robert Bailis*,[21] Lord Mayor, where I was sworn as not being a married Person, or an Apprentice by Indenture. He paid for my Oath one Shilling, a Perquisite[22] of his Clerk. From thence we went to *London-Bridge*, to a Stationer's Shop, and there an Indenture of Servitude was drawn, which I

19. Workers skilled in construction and agriculture and in making shoes and clothing were in great demand in most parts of America; see David W. Galenson, "Labor Market Behavior in Colonial America: Servitude, Slavery, and Free Labor," in David W. Galenson, ed., *Markets in History: Economic Studies of the Past* (Cambridge: Cambridge University Press, 1989), 65–66. Daniel Kent, an indentured servant who emigrated to Pennsylvania a half-century after Moraley, believed that similar occupations remained in demand in the region (Ella K. Barnard, comp., *Letters and Other Papers of Daniel Kent, Emigrant and Redemptioner* [Baltimore, 1904], 17).

20. A half crown equaled 2 shillings and 6 pence.

21. Robert Baylis was mayor from 1728 to 1729. See Alfred B. Beaven, *The Aldermen of the City of London, Temp. Henry III.—1912*, 2 vols. (London: Fisher, 1913), 2:124.

22. Something gained by a place or office in addition to wages.

sign'd.[23] After this we took {a} Boat at *Billingsgate*, steer'd our Course for *Limehouse*, where we arriv'd about Eleven o'Clock in the Forenoon. The Ship was named the *Bonetta*, of about 200 Tons; the Owner *Charles Hankin*, {and} *James Reed*, Commander. There were on board 20 Persons, all Men, bound to the same Place, and on the same Account. As soon as I enter'd, my Friend left me to think better on it, and wish'd me a prosperous Voyage, and a good Wife.

I observ'd several of my Brother Adventurers seem'd very dejected, from whence I guess'd they repented of their Rashness. Soon after, Dinner was brought on the Table, which consisted of stew'd Mutton Chops. I was very glad I had an Opportunity of trying the Temper of my Tusks, for I had not eaten any Meat for four Days. I eat very heartily, and wash'd down the mutton with about two Quarts of Small Beer.[24] I began to think myself happy, in being in a Way to eat; and on this Account, became insensible of the Condition I had brought myself to. In the Afternoon, the Master and Mate being absent, I ventur'd into the Cabin, and peeping into a Chest, discover'd a large Quantity of Raisins, of which I made free with about two Pound, and pocketed them for my own Use: Besides, the Small Beer stood upon Deck, and was free for us at all times; so that laying all Reflections {aside}, I comforted myself with the Hopes of living well all the Voyage, but was soon made sensible to the contrary when we set out to Sea.

23. The standard printed form for an indenture was as follows:

> London ff. These are to certify, that (name, residence, age, occupation) came before me one of His Majesty's Justices of Peace, and Voluntarily made Oath that (he/she) this Deponent (is) not Married, nor Apprentice nor Covenant, or Contracted Servant to any Persons, nor listed Soldier or Sailor in His Majesty's Service, and (is) free and willing to serve (agent's name) or his Assigns (#) Years in (place) His Majesty's Plantation in *America*, and that (he/she is) not perswaded, or enticed so to do, but that it is (his/her) own Voluntary Act.
>
> (signature of servant)
>
> Jurat (date)
> Coram me (signature of the justice of the peace)

Aside from stipulating the length of service, the standard contract provided no protections for the servant. Assurances of "necessary Cloaths, Meat, Drink, Washing and Lodging" appeared only in the contracts of minors. Additional guarantees for adult servants rarely were included. David Galenson, *White Servitude in Colonial America: An Economic Analysis* (Cambridge: Cambridge University Press, 1981), 200–203.

24. Beer with little alcoholic content.

The next Day I writ a Letter to one Mr *Stafford*, in *Old Fish-street*,[25] to let him know where I was, and whither bound. I sent it by the Mate's Wife, who deliver'd it to him. After he read the Letter, he bid her tell me, that I deserv'd all possible Hardships for my Imprudence, in leaving him at a time when he was doing me Justice, by prosecuting my Mother.

Three Days after, being under Sail, a Boat hail'd us, and the Boatman ask'd if there was not one *Moraley* on board. The Mate denied I was there; but was answer'd, there was an Order from the Lord Mayor to bring him back again. To which he replied, I was gone, the Captain having discharg'd me. So the Boatman was satisfied, and return'd. I was then fast asleep below, and the rest of the People were kept under Deck, to prevent their Knowlege of this Enquiry; which when I was made acquainted with, I curs'd my Fate ten thousand times.

That Evening we sail'd down the River for the *Nore*, and arriv'd at *Eriff*, where we took in fresh Provisions, and the next Morning anchor'd close to *Gravesend*. A Custom House Officer came on board, and demanded of us, one by one, whether we were forced against our Wills, or if we went voluntarily. There every Adventurer had his Apparel given him for the Voyage, which was, a Sea Jacket, two coarse chequ'd Shirts, a Woollen Waistcoat, two coarse Handkerchiefs, one Pair of Hose, a Woollen Cap, and a pair of bad new Shoes. Thus accoutr'd, we set Sail for *America*, with a fair Wind, on the 7th day of *September*, in the Year 1729.

The next Day we arriv'd at the *Downs*, and discover'd *Goodwin* Sand, and cast Anchor before *Deal* Castle.[26] The same Day the Captain mann'd a Boat for *Calais*, to buy Brandy. I begg'd of him to be one, for Curiosity's Sake; and after some Difficulty he granted me my Request. We arriv'd there after three Hours Sail, and on our Landing were civilly receiv'd by the Garrison. We bought a considerable Quantity of Brandy, they giving us a large Bowl of Punch for laying out Money. The Garrison at that Time consisted of 5000 Men, meanly clad, and as poorly

25. Old Fish Street was an extension of Knightrider Street and is now called by the latter name. See Eilert Ekwall, *Street-Names of the City of London* (Oxford: Clarendon Press, 1954), 74.

26. Ships often stopped at the town of Deal to take on supplies and to drop off the pilot. See Peter Kalm, *The America of 1750: Peter Kalm's Travels in North America*, ed. Adolph B. Benson, 2 vols. (New York: Dover, 1964), 1:1; and Edward Miles Riley, ed., *The Journal of John Harrower: An Indentured Servant in the Colony of Virginia, 1773–1776* (Williamsburg, Va.: Colonial Williamsburg, 1963), 29. See also Map 1.

fed. *Calais* is pretty strong by Art, made so purely to prevent a sudden Surprise from the *English*.

After two Hours Stay we return'd to the Ship, and the next Day perceiv'd *Goodwin* Sands beat higher than usual, which afforded a dismal Sight. Those Sands were once firm Land, adjoining to *Kent*, but were destroy'd in the Reign of *Edward* the Confessor[27] (about 700 Years ago), being then in the Possession of *Goodwin* Earl of *Kent*, Father to *Harold* II, King of *England*, but routed by *William*, Duke of *Normandy*, at the Battle of *Hastings*. Here we saw Droves of Purpoises playing in the Waves.

We then sail'd towards *Dover*, where we anchor'd. The Castle is a noble Range of Building. A Boat was sent off to fetch some more Provisions; which returning, brought on board three Gentlemen to see our Captain. One of them was nam'd *Sonds*, a Relation of Sir *George Sonds*.[28] He knew me at first Sight, and at my Desire related to the Company the unfortunate Story of Sir *George's* two Sons, which is as follows.

27. Edward the Confessor reigned from 1042 to 1066. William the Conqueror, victorious at the Battle of Hastings in 1066, became the first Norman monarch (1066–87).

28. Sir George Sondes, Earl of Feversham, 1600–1677, was the son of Sir Richard (not Michael) Sondes, and he was married in 1632 to Jane Freeman, daughter and heiress of Sir Ralph Freeman, Lord Mayor of London in 1633–34. The murder took place, as Moraley relates, on August 7, 1655. The case became celebrated as pamphleteers debated whether the father was the real culprit for having, as some claimed, "mismanaged his sons' education." See Leslie Stephen and Sidney Lee, eds., *Dictionary of National Biography*, 22 vols. (London: Oxford, 1917), 18:669–70.

2 THE STORY OF SIR GEORGE SONDS'S TWO SONS.

THIS Gentleman was the Son of Sir *Michael Sonds*, of *Lees Court*. He married the Daughter of Alderman *Freeman*, Lord Mayor of *London*; by her he had two Sons, the Elder named *George*, the Younger *Freeman*. His Estate was £*7000 per Ann.* in *Kent*, and at *Sonds-place*, in *Surrey*, he had £*2500 per Annum* more. His Sons had an Education suitable to their Birth, and after they had pass'd through their several Studies, remain'd with their Father, and for some time liv'd in the Bands of Amity; but an unlucky Accident disturb'd the Peace of the Family. The elder Brother fell in Love with a young Lady named *Anne Delaune*, Niece to Sir *George*, living with one Mr *Hugginson*, a Gentleman in the Neighbourhood, and a Relation. This Affair coming to the Father's Ears, he order'd his Son to leave off all Thoughts of such a Match, for that God would not bless it, on account of their Nearness of Blood. But he being under-hand solicited by the Lady's Friends, renew'd his Addresses; when Mr *Hugginson* acquainting his Father with it by Letter, he came to the House, and finding them together, laid his strict Commands on the Son not to proceed in his Amour, on pain of his Displeasure; then addressing himself to the Lady, said, He would get her a Husband in a proper Time. After this, Mr *George* not only left off all Conversation, but seem'd even to have an Aversion for her; and ever after was obedient to his Father.

About this Time young *Freeman* took a Fancy to a Lady, who was reported to have several Hundreds *per Annum*, and he proposed it to his Father; but he evading the Matter, made the Son the more assiduous, upon which his Father seemed to comply; but his Proposals not answering the Expectation of her Friends, the Match was broke of[f]: And Sir *George* telling him, he must think no more of Marriage, for he design'd him for the Inns of Court, where he should be well provided for, excited in him a disgust and hatred to his Brother, which caused frequent Quarrels between them; which the Father perceiving, told *Freeman*, that if he did not behave himself better to his Brother, he would disinherit him, as his Father had served his Uncle *Nicolas*; and that it was from his Brother he must expect his Fortune. This Discourse of the Father had no Effect on him, but from that Instant he formed a Design to kill his Brother that he might be the only Heir. One Night as they lay together he got out of Bed, and went into an adjoining Room, and took from thence a Cleaver and a Stilletto, a kind of Italian Poignard, with the first he clove his Head, and stabbed him in the Breast with the Stilletto; after which he went into his Father's Bed Chamber, and awaking him, said, *Sir, I have kill'd my Brother*. The Gentleman heard a Noise, but did not expect any such mischance, but arising, went with him into the Room, where he saw his Son not quite dead, weltering in his Blood. The next Morning the Affair got Wind. He was apprehended by the Officers of Justice, and committed to *Maidstone* Jail, where he remain'd along time till the Assizes, was then arraign'd for the Murder, which he confess'd, and became remarkable for his Repentance; but notwithstanding his Father's Interest, who got him repriev'd from time to time, he was hanged for the same; whereby an ancient noble Family, for want of direct Male Heirs, is extinct.

3 LIFE ON BOARD SHIP—STINTED RATIONS—DOLPHINS AND FLYING FISH—LAND AT LAST—IN THE MARKET—SOLD AS A SLAVE—"A QUAKER, BUT A WET ONE"—"THE ATHENS OF MANKIND"—GERMANTOWN.

THE Gentlemen being gone ashore, we soon after set sail for *Plymouth*; in two Days got into the Harbour, and anchor'd in *Cat Water*, where we moored our Ship. *Plymouth* is a strong Town, with a Fort, and Garrison, with four Companies of Soldiers. There one of our Adventurers made his escape, by swimming to Shore. We took in fresh Provision at this Place for the last time, a favourable Wind arising, we took the Advantage, and passed by *Eddistone* Lighthouse, steering our course toward the *Lizard* Point, which altered our Way of living for the Worse, for we were stinted in our Allowance, being joined together in Messes: Five to each Mess. Three Biscuits were given to each Man for the Day, and a small Piece of Salt Beef, no bigger then a Penny Chop of Mutton. Some Days we had Stockfish,[1] when every Man was obliged to

1. Dried cod, so called from its hardness.

beat his Share with a Maul to make it tender, with a little stinking Butter for Sauce.[2]

Every Morning and Evening the Captain called every one of us to the Cabbin Door, where we received a Thimble full of bad Brandy. We were obliged to turn out every four Hours, with the Sailors, to watch; which was to prevent our falling sick, by herding under Deck.

In our Voyage we observed little worth taking Notice of, till we were in Latitude 33,[3] when the Sun was intensely hot, which so partch'd our Bodies, having but a scanty Allowance of Water, not above three Quarts to each Mess. We attempted to drink the Salt Water, but it increased our Thirst. Sometimes, but rarely, it rained, when we set our Hats upon Deck to catch the Water; but it sliding down the Sails, gave it the Taste of Tarr.

We catched several Dolphins and flying Fish. They caught them thus: With a Weapon called by them a *Fizgig*, like the Fangs of *Neptune's* Trident, fixed to a long Pole and at the other End tied by a Rope fast to the Ship's Stern. When the Fish arrives near the Surface of the Water, they strike the Instrument downright, and having hooked the Fish, give it time to weary itself in the Water, to prevent his breaking the Line. For Goodness it surpasses a Cod.

The Dolphins Food is Flying Fish, who are so much afraid of them, that they scarce dare venture to dip themselves in the Water for fear of being caught by them, they being often oblig'd to wet their Wings, otherwise they would be dry, which prevents their Flying. They seldom rise above two or three Foot above the Surface, tho' I have seen them, when their Wings fail them, drop upon the Deck. They are about the Largeness of a Pilchard, and are good Food. I have eaten of them.

I had forgot the Magnitude of the Dolphins, they are generally one Foot and a Quarter long, flatter than a Salmon, and in the Water for Beauty exceed all the Fishes in the Ocean, having diversity of Colours,

2. Indentured servants sometimes received meager rations during the ocean voyage. John Harrower noted that the bondsmen on his ship almost mutinied when the captain initially notified them of their food allowance, and that two servants were shackled in irons for complaining about their diets during the voyage (*Journal of John Harrower*, 20). Farley Grubb, however, concluded that ship captains likely provided good dietary fare in order to deliver healthy servants who would bring a high price ("Redemptioner Immigration to Pennsylvania: Evidence on Contract Choice and Profitability," *Journal of Economic History* 46 [1986]: 407–18).

3. Latitude 33 runs north of Charleston, South Carolina, and south of Casablanca, Morocco.

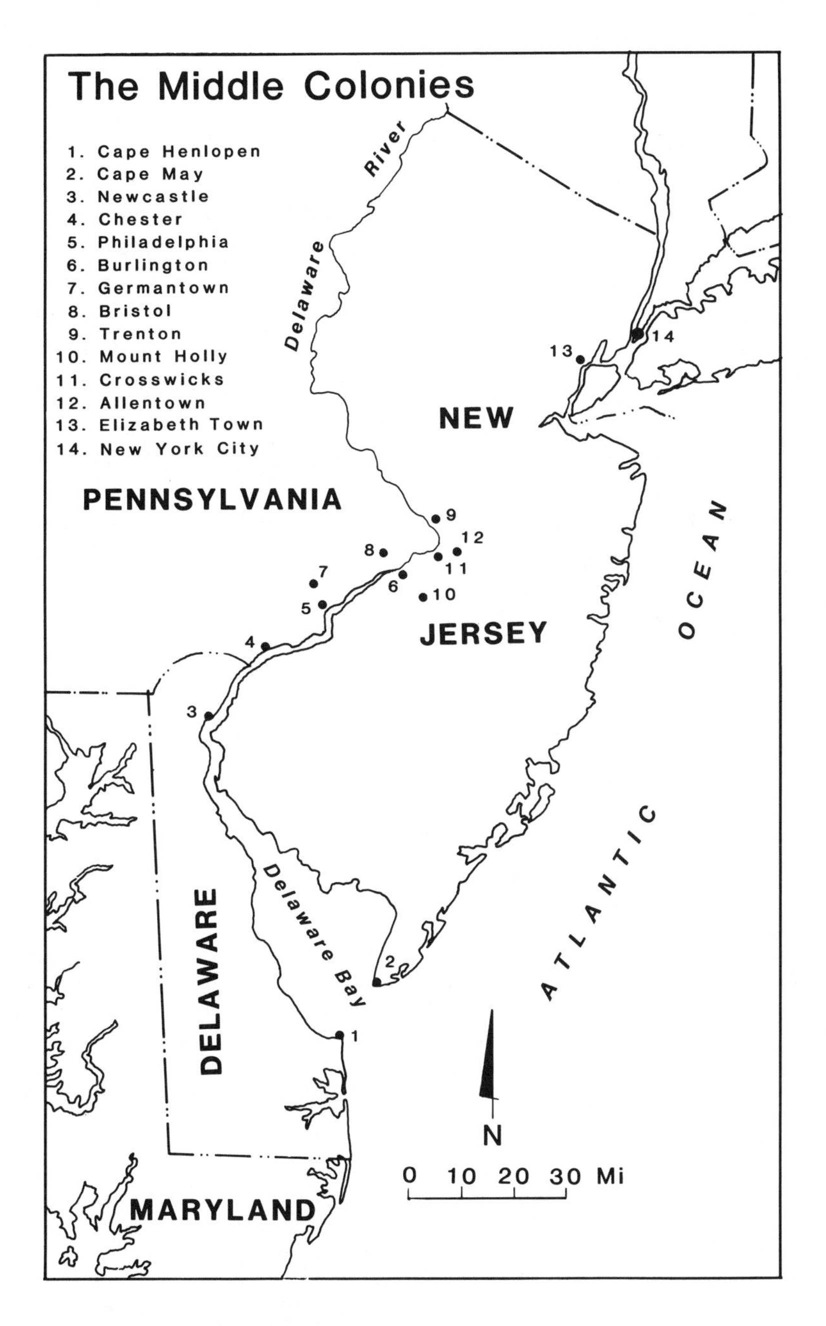

Map 2. The middle colonies.

of which Gold is the Principle, which by its shining, gives the flying Fish an Opportunity of avoiding them.

We saw several Land Birds at the Distance of fifteen hundred Miles from Land. When tired, they oftentimes alight on the Ship Masts, when they are easily taken. It is wonderful how they live so far from their proper Element, for when taken, being almost starved, they will eat unmercifully, but die soon after.

Every Day we discover'd a kind of Moss swimming upon the Sea, which plainly proved we were not far from the Gulph of *Mexico*, where it only grows.[4] We having hitherto used the Benefit of the *Monsoons*, or *Trade Winds*,[5] were obliged to steer for a more Northern Latitude, and very sensibly felt an Alteration in the Climate, which soon after became Cold. We got within Soundings, which we found by our Plummets, and discovered the *American* Coast, being *Cape Finlope*,[6] at the entrance of *Delaware* Bay, *Cape May* being opposite on the *New Jersey* Side.

We render'd God thanks for his Mercy in bringing us through so many Hardships, and prepair'd to sail up [the] *Delaware* River, so called from Capt. *Delaware*,[7] who first discovered it. In order to our more safe passing, there being many Rocks at the first Enterance, we took a Pilot; and in three Tides, after passing by *Newcastle* and *Chester*, arrived at *Philadelphia*, the day after *Christmas* Day.[8]

We drank so freely of the River Water, which, having a Purgative

4. The Sargasso Sea, characterized by the brown seaweed of its name, extends as far east as the Azores and is bounded on the west and north by the Gulf Stream.

5. The northeast trade winds would have carried the ship in a southwesterly direction toward the Caribbean, and the Westerlies would have carried it north along the North American coast.

6. Cape Henlopen, not Finlope, in Delaware (see Map 2).

7. Thomas West, third Lord de la Warr, landed briefly at the mouth of the river now bearing his name in 1611.

8. Moraley is mistaken about the date. The ship actually entered the port of Philadelphia during the week of December 9–16, 1729, according to reports in both the city's newspapers, the *Pennsylvania Gazette* (see Figure 7) and the *American Weekly Mercury*, for that week. Moraley thus spent thirteen weeks journeying from Gravesend to Philadelphia, about average for ocean passage at the time. After spending three weeks in Philadelphia, Moraley may have reached his new home in Burlington, New Jersey, on the day after Christmas, as he recalled. This chronology agrees with Moraley's subsequent comment that his first night in Burlington was the first time he had slept in a bed for fifteen weeks. Edward Horne and William Rawle, the two men who offered servants for sale from the ship on which Moraley arrived (see Figure 7), were Quaker merchants in the city (see Gary B. Nash, "The Early Merchants of Philadelphia," in Richard S. Dunn and Mary Maples Dunn, eds., *The World of William Penn* [Philadelphia: University of Pennsylvania Press, 1986], 360–61). The *Boneta* left Philadelphia for London during the first week of the new year, according to the *Pennsylvania Gazette* and the *American Weekly Mercury*, December 30–January 6, 1730, issues.

Cuſtom-Houſe, Philadelphia, Entred inwards.
Ship Amity, William Murray, from Jamaica.
Ship Boneta, Thomas Read, from London.
Entred Outwards.
Brig. Philadelphia Hope, G. Spafford, for Weſt-Indies.
Sloop Surinam, Henry Norwood, for Barbadoes.
Cleared Out.
Sloop Adventure, Robert Rawle, to Surinam.
Ship Samuel and Ann, Thomas Glentworth, to Madera.
Brigt. Clementina, Joſeph Arthur, to Antigua.
Brigt. Henrietta, Samuel Farra, to Madera.
Ship Cupid, Stephen Pugh, to Gibraltar.
Ship Three Batchelors, William Spafford, to Barbadoes.
Ship Mary, Robert Sanders, to Iſle of Man.
Buried in the ſeveral Burying-Grounds ſince the 4th Inſtant.
Church ---------- 2. Baptiſts ---------- 0.
Quakers ---------- 1. Strangers, Whites ---------- 0.
Presbyterians ---------- 0. Blacks ---------- 0.

A D V E R T I S E M E N T S.

JUſt Imported in the Ship *Boneta*, Capt. *Thomas Reed*, Maſter, from *London*, (lying near the Market Wharff) a Parcel of very likely Servant Men and Boys, of ſundry Trades, as well as Husbandmen: To be ſold by *Edward Horne* and *William Rawle*, very Reaſonable, (as alſo good *Newcaſtle* Coal) for Caſh, Flower or Bread.

Figure 7. Newspaper notice of the arrival of the ship *Boneta* and advertisement of servants for sale, *Pennsylvania Gazette* (Philadelphia), December 9–16, 1729. Moraley arrived on this ship and was among the servants advertised to be sold.

Quality, caused some of us to fall Sick. I got a Diabates,[9] that brought me so low, that being reduced to a very weak Condition, I was forced to drink Rum, which drying up and strengthening the urinary Vessels, after three Months was cured.

We all of us had the Liberty of Visiting the Town, where I sold my

9. "Diabetes" is a term meaning the excessive production of urine. Samuel Johnson defined it as "a morbid copiousness of urine; a fatal colliquation by the urinary passages." It is now associated with either diabetes mellitus, caused by insufficient insulin production of the pancreas, or diabetes insipidus, a disorder of the pituitary gland. None of these descriptions fits Moraley's problem, which he claims to have cured through three months of drinking rum.

Red Coat for a Quart of Rum, my Tie Wig for Sixpence, with which I bought a Three-penny Loaf, and a Quart of Cyder.[10] Our Cargo consisting chiefly of Voluntary Slaves, who are the least to be pitied, I saw all my Companions sold of[f] before me; my turn came last, when I was sold for eleven Pounds, to one Mr *Isaac Pearson*,[11] a Man of Humanity, by Trade a Smith, Clock-maker and Goldsmith, living at *Burlington*, in *New Jersey*: He was a Quaker, but a Wet one.[12]

During my stay at *Philadelphia*, which was three Weeks, I had an Opportunity to survey one of the most delightful Cities upon Earth. As I was one Day amusing myself with the Prospect from the Water, being in a Poetick Strain, I hammered out the following Rhyme. The Reader must not expect from me a fine Performance, but such as it is, I freely give.[13]

10. That Moraley was allowed to leave the ship and wander about the city before he was sold was not typical. Just one year earlier a few servants absconded while roving around Philadelphia before they were auctioned, prompting most captains to confine servants to their ships until they had been purchased. See Farley Grubb, "The Auction of Redemptioner Servants, Philadelphia, 1771–1804: An Economic Analysis," *Journal of Economic History* 45 (1985): 585.

11. Isaac Pearson (ca. 1685–1749) was a blacksmith, silversmith, goldsmith, button manufacturer, ironmaster, and master watchmaker and clockmaker. Active in politics, he served as a state assemblyman, as state assay master for weights and measures, and as seal master. He married Hannah Gardiner in 1710, and they had three daughters, Rebecca, Elizabeth, and Sarah, who survived to adulthood. In 1746, he wed Rebecca Lovett, the widow of Samuel Scattergood, and she brought five minor children to the marriage. See Charles J. Burton, "A New Jersey Clock," *Bulletin of the National Association of Watch and Clock Collectors* 8 (1958): 213–14; Julia Sabine, "Silversmiths of New Jersey, 1623–1800," *Proceedings of the New Jersey Historical Society* 61 (1943): 252–55; Charles S. Boyer, *Early Forges and Furnaces in New Jersey* (Philadelphia: University of Pennsylvania Press, 1931), 128–29; William E. Drost, *Clocks and Watches of New Jersey* (Elizabeth, N.J.: Engineering Publishers, 1966), 192–201; and Carl M. Williams, *Silversmiths of New Jersey, 1700–1825, with Some Notice of Clockmakers Who Were Also Silversmiths* (Philadelphia: McManus, 1949), 34–45. See also "An Analysis of the Isaac Pearson Tall Clock in the Vauxhall Room, Winterthur," report from the Winterthur Museum Library, Delaware, May 1986; and Elaine Brenchley, "Isaac Pearson: Clockmaker of Burlington, West Jersey," Apprentice Guide Paper, Winterthur Museum Library, June 1982, both photocopied typescripts deposited at the Burlington County Historical Society. See Figure 14 for a clock produced in Pearson's shop.

12. A "wet" Quaker was a worldly member of the Society of Friends, a person whose behavior was not as austere, plain, and spiritual as those who adhered more strictly to the faith. Gaiety and attention to fashion characterized many wet Quakers. See Frederick B. Tolles, *Meeting House and Counting House: The Quaker Merchants of Colonial Philadelphia, 1682–1783* (Chapel Hill: University of North Carolina Press, 1948), 142–43.

13. Moraley cribbed most of this poem from one written by George Webb that appeared in Titan Leed, *The Genuine Leed's Almanac for . . . 1730* (Philadelphia: Leeds, 1730). However, Moraley shortened, rewrote, and added some original lines to the poem. On Webb, see David S. Shields, "The Wits and Poets of Pennsylvania: New Light on the Rise of Belles Lettres in Provincial Pennsylvania, 1720–1740," *PMHB* 109 (1985): 122–33. See also Appendix D for a full version of the original poem.

Key:

1. The Governours House
2. Quakers Meeting
3. The Market House
4. Where the Ships are built
5. Coopers Ferry
6. The Island
7. Society Hill
8. Wickacove
9. The Sweeds Church
10. Part of Gloster

Figure 8. "The Prospect of Philadelphia from Wickacove, exactly Delineated by G. Wood" (G. Wood, 1735). Although somewhat fanciful, this is the sole surviving depiction of the city at the time of Moraley's journey.

Goddess of Numbers, who art wont to rove
O'er the gay Landskip, and the smiling Grove:
Assist the soaring Muse, with Judgment to repeat.
The various Beauties of Thy Fav'rite Seat;
Thy Streets and Lanes, how regular and fair,
With thee no earthly City may compare.
While *Europe* groans, distress'd by hostile War,
No fears disturb the industrious Planters Care:
No unjust Sentence we have cause to fear;
No arbitrary Monarch rules us here.
Our Laws, our Liberties, and all are ours,
Our happy Constitution here secures,
The Seers, how cautious! and how gravely wise!
The hopeful Youth in Emulation rise;
Who, if the aspiring Muse does rightly sing,
Shall liberal Arts to such Perfection bring,
That *Europe* shall mourn, her antient Fame declin'd,
And *Philadelphia* shall be the *Athens* of Mankind.
What Praise, O Pen![14] what Thanks are due to thee!
For this first perfect Scheme of Liberty!
What Praise! what Thanks! to thee, O Pen! are given,
Beloved of Men! and Candidate for Heaven.

This famous City, is in the 40 Degree of Northern Latitude, and seated close to the Banks of [the] *Delaware*, which is here above one Mile broad,[15] and affords a fine Prospect on both Sides of it, there being great Numbers of fine Seats along its Banks, surrounded by pleasant Walks, and great Variety of different Sorts of Land, as Woods, Groves, verdant Fields, and Meadows. The Town stands on level Ground, which extends to seven or eight Miles in Circumference:[16] A charming Country it is, producing the most delectable Fruits of different Kinds, which

14. William Penn (1644–1718) was Proprietor of Pennsylvania from 1681 until his death.

15. The Delaware River at Market Street is still almost three-quarters of a mile broad, but the shores have been extended by developers since Moraley's day. Peter Kalm, a Swedish scientist, estimated the width of the Delaware River at Philadelphia as three-quarters of a mile in 1748 (Kalm, *America of 1750*, 1:27).

16. Moraley overestimates the city's circumference, which was probably much closer to three or four miles.

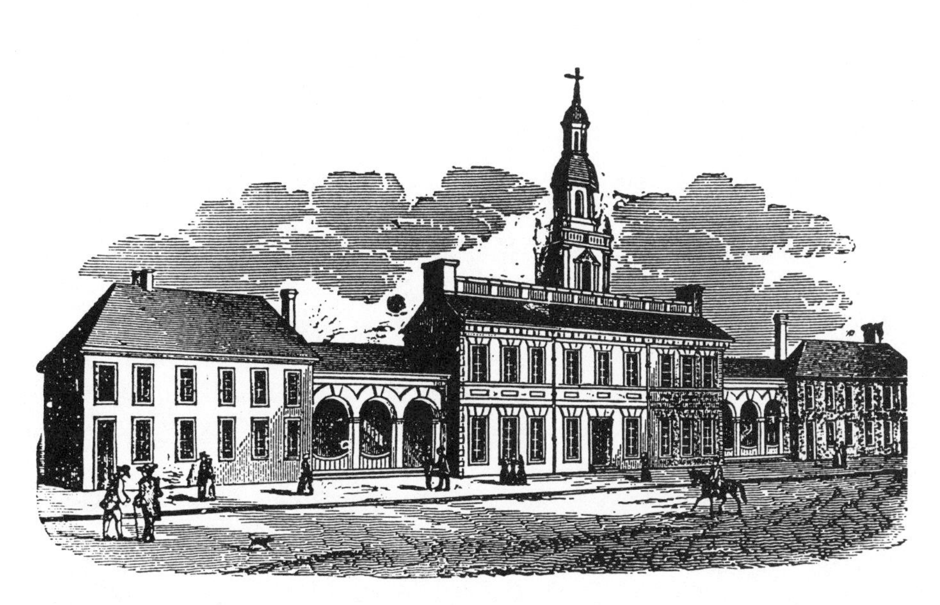

Figure 9. The Old Provincial State House, Philadelphia.

Figure 10. Christ Church, Philadelphia.

grow in great Abundance, and are common to the weary Traveller, as well as the wealthy Citizen, it being no Trespass to gather them.

There are many Houses of Entertainment, at convenient distance from the Town, where the Inhabitants resort, in the cool Evenings, after the Fatigues of Business, where they regale themselves with the Product of this fertile Soil. This City is as large as *Bristol*, in *England*, but not so populous; and contains about 25,000 People,[17] who have Shops and Houses as handsome as those at *Newcastle upon Tyne*. The Streets are long and strait, and are called by these Names, *First Street, Second Street, Third Street, Fourth Street, Water Street*, lying along the Water, *Chestnut Street, Walnut Street, Front Street*, beside a good Number of Allies; as, *Mulberry Ally, Strawberry Ally, Black Horse Ally*, &c.

At the Upper-End of *Second Street*, is a State House,[18] for the Meeting of the Governor and Assembly, but not quite finished when I was there, which when done would be the finest Edifice in all *America*. The Market-place has a handsome House in it, where the Assembly sat, till the other was finished; this Fronts the River. In the Shambles[19] of this Market are sold all Kinds of Butchers Meat, as well cut and drest as at *London*: The Market Days are *Wednesdays* and *Saturdays*; but they have a Custom of retaling their Meat on *Sundays*, which is observed all over *America* in the Summer Time, because of the Heat of the Weather; Hens, Chickens, and Wild Fowl, are vended, with Poultry of all Kinds, and Fruits and Herbs.

The Houses are all of Brick, well sashed and glazed, and covered with white Cedar, more durable than Tiles.[20] The Oldest House in the Place, when I was there, being not above 49 Years standing. The Mayor has the Management of the Affairs, as chief Magestrate; but if he refuse to

17. The city and suburbs contained approximately 8,000 inhabitants in 1734. See Billy G. Smith, "Death and Life in a Colonial Immigrant City: A Demographic Analysis of Philadelphia," *Journal of Economic History* 37 (1977): 863–83; and P. M. G. Harris, "The Demographic Development of Colonial Philadelphia in Some Comparative Perspective," in Susan E. Klepp, ed., *The Demographic History of the Philadelphia Region, 1600–1860* (Philadelphia: American Philosophical Society, 1989), also published as a volume in *Proceedings of the American Philosophical Society* 133 (1989): 262–304.

18. Construction on the State House, now better known as Independence Hall, was begun in 1732, but the building was not occupied until 1741. See Edwin B. Bronner, "Village into Town, 1701–1746," in Russell F. Weigley, ed., *Philadelphia: A 300-Year History* (New York: W. W. Norton, 1982), 52–53.

19. Slaughterhouse.

20. Moraley exaggerates here, because many of the city's homes were constructed of stone or wood (Kalm, *America of 1750*, 1:19–20). Not until 1795 did a city ordinance require that buildings in the center of the city must be fabricated of brick.

Figure 11. Stone Prison, southwest corner of Third and High Streets, Philadelphia.

do Justice, an Appeal lyes against him, to the Governor, who never fails to do Justice, he being a Man of an universal Character: He is a *Scotchman*, by Name *Gordon*,[21] and was a Major in Queen *Anne's* Army.[22]

The Religion professed here is of several Kinds: The *Establish'd* has the Preheminence, and has a large Church with an Organ. The *Quakers*, singly, are the most Numerous, who have two large Meetings; but if the *Presbyterians, Independents, Baptists, Papists* and *Freethinkers*, be joined to the Church Party, then the *Quakers* are not half the Number of the Inhabitants.[23]

21. Major Patrick Gordon served as the lieutenant governor of Pennsylvania from 1726 to 1736.

22. Queen Anne reigned from 1702 to 1714.

23. By "Establish'd" Moraley means the Church of England, although that church enjoyed no special legal status under Pennsylvania law. The Anglicans began construction of Christ Church (see Figure 10) in 1727 and completed it in 1744. The Quakers (Society of Friends) may have formed the largest religious group in the county, but burial statistics indicate that the number of Church of England members in the city was larger. The Presbyterians encompassed various English-speaking Calvinist groups, while the Baptists were a long-established but small congregation in the city. The "Papists," or Roman Catholics, had held services in Philadelphia since 1720, but they did not build a chapel until 1733. "Freethinkers" were not attached to any church and, based on burial statistics for 1730–32, accounted for as much as one-third of the population. Slaves comprised many of the residents not affiliated with any church. Moraley ignores the non-British religious groups, such as the Swedish Lutheran, German Lutheran, and German Reformed congregations active in the city at this time. See Bronner, "Village into Town," 47–53; and Susan E. Klepp, *"The Swift Progress of Population": A Documentary and Bibliographic Study of Philadelphia's Growth* (Philadelphia: American Philosophical Society, 1991), 46–47.

Here is a Lodge of the Society of Free and Accepted Masons. The principal Houses are Mr *Andrew Hamilton's*,[24] a *Scotch* Gentleman, who retired from *Scotland* for unfortunately killing his Brother[, and] *Israel Pemberton*,[25] a wealthy Quaker, of great Probity. The Post House is kept by Mr *Andrew Bradford*,[26] where he has a Printing House. At the End of the Town is *Society Hill*,[27] a pleasant Place, and a House of Entertainment, where I have spent many a Pound; it lies in the Road to *Scuylkill*.[28] I had forgot the Prison, a neat Stone Building, having but little of that look.

Here are three Watchmakers Shops; Mr *Peter Stretch* is the most eminent; next to him *John Wood*, then *Edmund Lewis*,[29] a brisk young Quaker, a Lover of *Supernaculum*.[30] They have two Fairs in the Years, when all Sorts of Household Furniture and Toys are sold. No Saints Days nor other Holidays are observed, except the First of *November*, the King's Birth-day and *Christmas Day*, by the Church People.

The Key for landing Goods is large and convenient, with Wharfs and Warehouses, stor'd with plenty of *European* Commodities, here being always at least 40 Ships of good Burthen in the River, and many are built after the *English* Fashion, the Woods producing Timber for that Purpose.

In the Summer time, People seldom wear Wigs, but thin Caps under

24. Andrew Hamilton (1676–1741), lawyer and Speaker of the Assembly, originally called himself Trent when he arrived in America. The reason for his change of name and the secrecy concerning his earlier life is unknown, although one rumor was that he had killed a lord in a duel. His estate, Bush Hill, was located just outside Philadelphia. See J. Thomas Scharf and Thomas Westcott, *History of Philadelphia, 1609–1884*, 3 vols. (Philadelphia: Everts, 1884), 2:1501–2.

25. Israel Pemberton (1684–1754) was a wealthy Quaker merchant (ibid., 2:1251).

26. Andrew Bradford (1686–1742) published the first newspaper in Pennsylvania, the *American Weekly Mercury*. See Anna Janney DeArmond, *Andrew Bradford, Colonial Journalist* (Newark: University of Delaware Press, 1949).

27. Society Hill received its name from the Free Society of Traders, an early corporation that by 1723 had ceased operations.

28. The Schuylkill River is slightly more than two miles west of Society Hill.

29. Both Peter Stretch (1670–1746) and John Wood (Sr.) (d. 1761) were established clockmakers with shops on Front Street in Philadelphia; both also had sons who would become accomplished Philadelphia clockmakers. See James W. Gibbs, *Pennsylvania Clocks and Watches: Antique Timepieces and Their Makers* (University Park: The Pennsylvania State University Press, 1984), 69–73, 79–81. Edmund Lewis left few traces in the city's records; perhaps he was the Edmund Lewis who apprenticed as a clockmaker in London for seven years in 1727 but who never completed his apprenticeship (see Atkins, *Register of Apprentices*, 180). Lewis presented a removal certificate from the New York monthly Meeting of Friends, recorded in Philadelphia on March 25, 1732 (Abstracts of Minutes, Philadelphia Monthly Meeting, vol. 3: 1730–85, p. 14, GSP).

30. A liquor to be drunk to the last drop, hence, alcohol of good quality.

their Hats, and without Coats, frequently going to Church without them. The Negroes and bought Servants, are clad in coarse Osnabrigs,[31] both Coat, Waistcoat, Breeches, and Shirt, being of the same Piece, and so rough, that the Shirt occasions great Uneasiness to the Body. This Wearing generally costs from fifteen to twenty Pence a Yard.

Four Miles from *Philadelphia* lies *German Town*,[32] so call'd because built and inhabited by the *Palatines*. It is a large Place, well contrived. These People are supposed to be 40,000 in *Pensilvania* only,[33] and behave themselves so well, as gains them the Respect of the *English*; and are ready, in case of an Invasion, to appear in the Defence of the Province, and frequently exercise themselves at their Arms. They have many considerable Farms, which they improve to the best Advantage: Many of them are naturaliz'd by Law, which enables them to purchase Lands, and capacitates them to hold Places in the Government. Since the first Settling of these People, not one of them have suffered the Law for any Offence.

During my Stay here, I had an Opportunity of conversing with a *Spanish* Gentleman who related to me his Adventures, which for their Singularity, I shall relate in his own Words.

31. A cheap, coarse, strong linen originally made in Oznabrug, Germany, and commonly worn by the lower classes in England and America (Peter F. Copeland, *Working Dress in Colonial and Revolutionary America* [Westport, Conn.: Greenwood Press, 1977], 204). See Figure 16 for a drawing of the type of clothing worn by slaves.

32. Germantown had a population of 340 in 1734 (Stephanie G. Wolf, *Urban Village: Population, Community, and Family Structure in Germantown, Pennsylvania, 1683–1800* [Princeton: Princeton University Press, 1976], 43).

33. About 52,000 people lived in Pennsylvania in 1730, while an additional 9,000 lived in Delaware, which was then under the jurisdiction of Pennsylvania (U.S. Bureau of the Census, *Historical Statistics of the United States, Colonial Times to 1970*, 2 vols. [Washington, D.C.: Department of Commerce, Bureau of the Census, 1976], 2:1168). The colony contained approximately 23,000 Germans in 1727, and about 2,300 arrived in Philadelphia's port between 1727 and 1730 (Marianne Wokeck, "The Flow and Composition of German Immigration to Philadelphia, 1727–1775," *PMHB* 105 [1981]: 259–60).

MY Name is *Alonso Tellez de Almenara*, of *Sevile*, Capital of *Andalousia*, in *Spain*, where I had a competent Fortune left me by my Father, which I considerably improved by trading to *Mexico*; but marrying unhappily, I became involved in Debt: The best Part of my Estate was sold for the Discharge of them; and with the Remainder I was resolved to seek my Fortune. After I had maturely considered to what Place I should go, I pitched upon *Hispaniola*. I agreed with *Don Silvia de Mendora* for my Passage. He was Commander of the *Esperance*, a Man of War of 50 Guns. I was a Voluntier. We sailed from *Cadiz* in 1710.

Three Days after we discover'd a Sail, and presently perceived, it was a Corsair of *Barbary*: Upon which the Captain called all Hands upon Deck, and prepared to give them a vigorous Reception. On their nearer Approach, we found them to be of superior Force to us; but being resolved to defend ourselves to the last, rather than submit to *Barbarian* Slavery, the Corsair began with us by a Broadside, which we returned, fighting it out with unparallell'd Bravery. But most of our Men being killed in the Engagement, we were obliged to strike to them, after an Hour and a half's Conflict; when they boarded us, and proceeded to rummage our Ship. I lost my Cargo consisting of about Eight Thousand Pieces of Eight, and all my Wearing Apparel. The Captain was plundered to the Value of 40,000 Pieces of Eight.

No sooner was the Hurry over, but all the valuable Effects were removed on board the Corsair, with myself and the remainder of the Crew, being only five Persons, the Slain, being nine in Number, were thrown over board. We were secured under Hatches, and the Ship steered its Course for *Sallee*,[1] a Piratical Port in the *Atlantick* Ocean, where we arrived in five Days. After some time we were set on Shore, in order to be presented to the King of *Morocco*, all Slaves brought into his Ports, being his Property.

After a short Stay, during which we were put into a Dungeon under Ground, by the *Moors* called *Mazmarra's*, we were conducted by Land towards *Miquenez*,[2] chief City of that Prince's Dominions, at about 36 Miles distance from *Sallee*; in the Kingdom of *Fez*.[3]

At our first Arrival we were presented every one of us with a Chain of twenty three Pounds Weight, which was fastened about our legs, and then were put into one of these Dungeons spoken of before, where was no Light, nor any Thing to sit upon. Our Food was *Cous Cous*, a Hasty Pudding made of Corn and Water.

After three Days Imprisonment, we were led out to be presented to the King, who about Eleven in the Morning, attended by about six hundred Blacks of his Guard, came to view the Works he was raising adjoining to his Pallace. He carefully examined our Physognomy, and observing one of us who seemed to be fearful, spoke to him in the *Moorish* Tongue, and demanded of him, if he would change his Religion, and become *Moor*. The Man answer'd in *Spanish*, he was resolved to die in the Religion of the Christians; which brave Speech so irritated this Prince, that, without speaking one Word more, he darted his Javelin at him, and struck him dead at his Feet. We all trembling, expected the same Fate.

After this Execution, he ordered us to be led to the Works. We

1. Located on the Atlantic coast of Morocco, Salé was a noted center for the corsairs.

2. During the late seventeenth century the Moroccan sultan used 30,000 workers, including at least 2,000 Christian captives, to construct the city of Meknes. See Ellen G. Friedman, *Spanish Captives in North Africa in the Early Modern Age* (Madison: University of Wisconsin Press, 1983), 67.

3. Fez was a town located in the interior of Morocco, approximately 125 miles east of Salé.

thought ourselves happy in escaping; so we were forced to climb up Ladders and Scaffolds loaden with Mortar and Timber besides our Chains, that before Evening we were so wearied, as is impossible to express: After Sun set we were conducted to our Prison. This Life I lived for one Year, in which time I have been Witness to above a Thousand Murders committed by this Inhuman Prince.

About this Time he meditated a War against the King of *Algiers*,[4] which Kingdom he fancied he might very easily add to his own, and passed the River *Meluya*, the *Mulucha* of *Sallust*, which divides the Kingdom of *Fez* from that of *Algiers*, with 60,000 Men, raw and undiciplin'd, mostly armed with Clubs and Javelins. I was in the Expedition. We marched towards *Tremezen*, a City not far from Mount *Atlas*, formerly Head of a Kingdom of the same Name, of about two Hundred Miles in Length, now added to *Algier*, which, with some Part of *Tunis* added, makes *Algier* the largest of the Kingdoms of *Barbary*.

We arrived at *Tremezen* six Days after our Setting out, but the *Algerines* were before us with 12,000 Men, Veteran Troops, who, without giving us time to put ourselves in Order of Battle, attacked us so vigorously, as compelled us to leave the Field, with 5000 Men killed, and 2000 made Prisoners. The Alcade that commanded was obliged to retire, and repass the River *Meluya*, and lost his Head for his Mismanagement.

I was soon after recommended to the King's Favour, and preferred to the Post of Receiver of the Taxes in the Province of *Tremezen*, so was freed from my Chain. I had an Opportunity of observing the Country, which is a fine one; but the Natives not having any Property, all being the King's, the Land lies uncultivated. From my first Advancement I formed several Projects to escape, but the Attempt being dangerous, I was cautious how I proceeded, and continu'd quiet two Years, when a Quantity of Gold being in my Custody, which I collected for the King's Use, I secured about forty Pounds Weight, with which I was resolved to leave the Place, when I had the least to fear.

On the twenty first Day of July, 1713, accompanied by a *French* Slave, I set out in the Night for *Ceuta*.[5] We travell'd all Night, and in the Day concealed ourselves in the Woods and Desarts, for fear of

4. A city-state east of Morocco.

5. On the northwest tip of Africa, Ceuta had been controlled by the Spanish for more than a century.

Lyons, Leopards, and other Beasts of Prey; and, to prevent discovery by the *Moors* and *Arabs*, we carefully avoided the Adours or Villages, and frequently saw the *Carracans*, but always had the good Luck not to be seen.

After five Nights ranging about, having no Guide but a Pocket Compass, we discovered in the Morning the Steeples of *Ceuta*, and the *Moorish* Army before the Town. We were sadly perplexed how we should pass the Camp, when suddenly the *Spaniards* made a Sally, and attacked the *Moors* so bravely, that they fled with the utmost Percipitation. The *Spaniards* pursued them, with so much Eagerness, that they left the Town two Leagues, and in coming back, a Party of them discovered us, and brought us into the Town, where we were congratulated upon our Deliverance. This Town is always blocked up by the *Moors*, by which Means they drive a Trade with the *Europeans*, for Guns and Gun-powder.

After I had remained with the Garrison sometime, I went on board a *French* Ship bound to *Malaga*; from whence I rode to *Seville*, and made myself known to my Friends, and was reconciled to my Wife, who in my Absence had, by the Wine Trade, acquired about 6000 Livres. I lived some Years with her in Love and Unity, after which she died, which threw me into a Melancholy; but it wearing off, I was resolved once more to settle in the *West Indies*, and sailed on board a Man of War to that Intent.

Our Voyage was prosperous, and we reached the appointed Place, which was St *Augustine* in *Florida*: But finding I was mistaken as to the Advantages I at first proposed, sailed for *Mexico*, but the Wind proving treacherous, by stress of Weather, we were drove upon the Coasts of the *English* Settlements, and anchor'd in *Chisapeak Bay*; where being informed of the Advantages I might meet from the generous Inhabitants, I went to *Philadelphia*, where I have lived many Years, and have, by Trade, acquired above one hundred thousand Pounds. I married an *English* Woman of Fortune, who is now living here: By her I have had some Children; I have an Opportunity of conversing with the Protestants of all Denominations, and comparing their Manners with the Catholicks, publickly renounced the Errors of the *Romish* Church and embraced that of the Church of *England*, in which I am resolved to continue.

5 BURLINGTON—CHURCHES AND MISSIONARIES—QUAKER MEETINGS—THE MAYOR OF PHILADELPHIA—RESCUING A LADY—AN EXCHANGE OF WIT—A NEGRO'S GHOST—THE DELAWARE RIVER—PERRIWIG ISLAND—AN ENORMOUS SKELETON—ANTEDILUVIAN REMAINS.

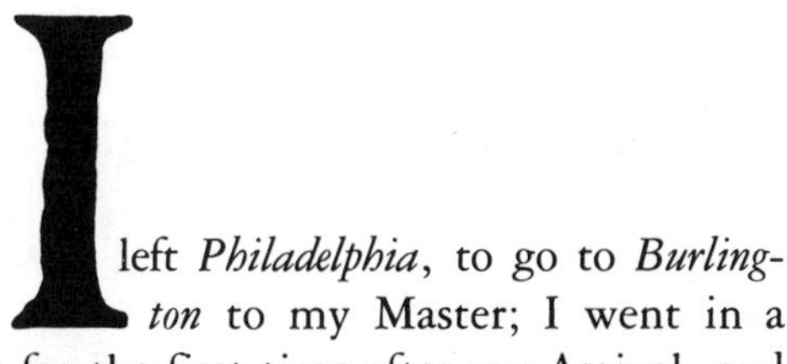

I left *Philadelphia*, to go to *Burlington* to my Master; I went in a Boat, where I got my self Drunk for the first time after my Arrival, and then first experienced the Strength of Rum. About Twelve we landed there, and I was conveyed to my Master, where I dined upon Dumplings, boil'd Beef, and Udder; when I became enamour'd with Mrs *Sarah*,[1] the Daughter. I was stripp'd of my Rags, and received in lieu of them a torn Shirt, and an old Coat. They tell me, it was only for the present, for I might expect better.

I went to bed that Night, being the first Time I had seen one since I left *London*, which was fifteen Weeks. The next day I had leave, upon

1. The title "Mrs" indicates Sarah Pearson's superior social station as the daughter of Moraley's master, not her marital status. Sarah Pearson would wed Joseph Hollinshead, who apprenticed under her father, in 1740. Hollinshead became Isaac Pearson's partner immediately after the marriage and inherited the clockmaking business when Pearson died. Hollinshead is mentioned in Williams, *Silversmiths of New Jersey*, 39–41; see also William Wade Hinshaw, *Encyclopedia of American Quaker Genealogy*, 9 vols. (Richmond, Ind.: Edwards, 1938), 2:249.

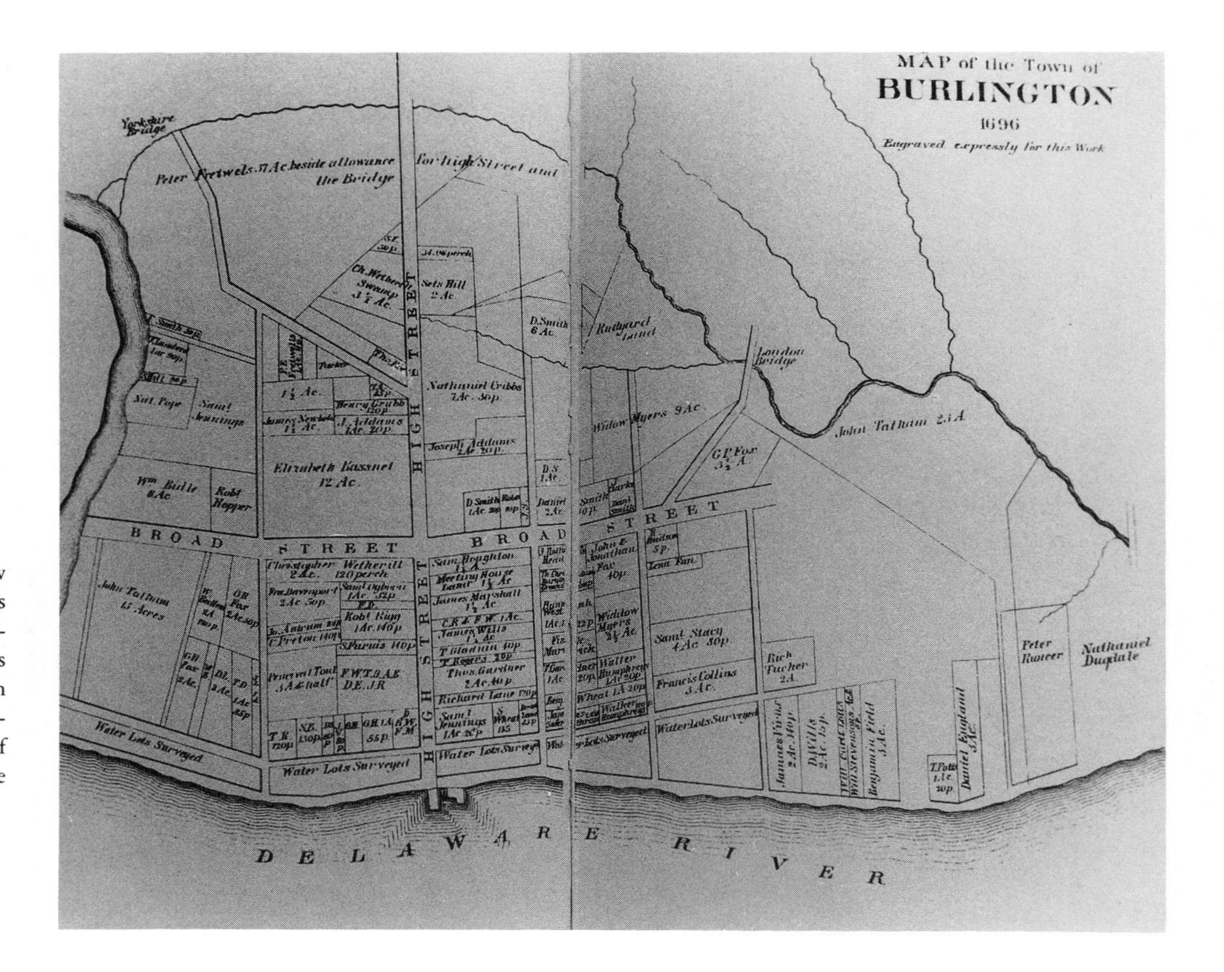

Map 3. Burlington, New Jersey, 1696. Moraley's master, Isaac Pearson, purchased the estate of James Wills on High Street in 1715. Here Moraley believed he saw the ghost of the murdered African slave in 1730.

Figure 12. Friends' Meeting House, Burlington, New Jersey, 1683.

Figure 13. Old St. Mary's Church, Burlington, New Jersey. Built in 1702.

my Desire, to walk about the Town: It is close to the River, and contains about 300 Houses; the Number of inhabitants was 800. It has a Key and Wharf, where Ships of 500 Tun may anchor: At the Upper-End, is the Prison, built of Brick.[2] Every House has a Garden and Orchard, stored with Apples, Peaches, and Cherries. Cyder is the common Drink here; some Houses making one hundred and fifty Barrels in the Year.

There are two Quaker Meetings, and one Church, which is of Brick, with a low Steeple; it is neat, and well contrived: The Incumbent, when I was there, was the Rev. Mr *Wayman*, a *Welshman*, a Gentleman of Parts, and the most extensive Goodness.[3] Since I have mentioned him, I think it necessary to say something of the State of the Church in these Parts. All the *British* Colonies are in the Diocess of *London*, and consequently the Bishop of that Place is Superintendant in Ecclesiastical Cases, who sends Missionaries to keep up a Vissibility of the Christian Faith, and to instruct the Natives; but I believe little Pains is taken with them.

The Sallaries settled on them as Missionaries, is fifty Pounds *English* yearly, and sent them in Vendible Goods, and brings them, by a right Management, £300 *per Cent*. This with the Cheapness of Provisions, enables the Clergy to keep up a good Figure, and frees them from Contempt. The Perquisites of their Profession brings them but little, because their *Easter* Offerings are but indifferently paid; and the other Branch of their Business, Matrimony, is disputed with them by the Magistrates, who marry as well as they. The Reason, I conceive, is, because of the great Distance of the Parishes, which makes it very chargable, and inconvenient in travelling, when a Justice can answer the End as well.

2. Located about twenty miles from Philadelphia, Burlington may have been even smaller than Moraley believed (see Map 3). Another contemporary indicated that "Burlington is situate on the River *Delaware*, is the Capital Town of that Division, called *West-Jersey*, containing above 200 families: the Place honoured with the Courts being kept here, the Houses were neatly built of Brick, and the Markets well supplied with Provisions." David Humphreys, *An Historical Account of the Incorporated Society for the Propagation of the Gospel in Foreign Parts* (London: Downing, 1730), 182. Nearly two decades later Peter Kalm observed that Burlington did not rival Philadelphia as a port town (Kalm, *America of 1750*, 1:321). Its importance continued to decline through the century. According to one report in 1780, Burlington contained only 160 houses and a total population of 1,110 (E. M. Woodward and John F. Hageman, *History of Burlington and Mercer Counties, New Jersey* [Philadelphia: Everts & Peck, 1883], 163).

3. The Reverend Robert Wayman served as rector of St. Mary's Church in Burlington (Figure 13) from 1730 to 1737.

Figure 14. Clock from the shop of Isaac Pearson, William Moraley's master.

On the other Side of the River lies *Bristol*, in *Bucks* County, in *Pensilvania*, larger than *Burlington*; but has little remarkable in it, but is the Post Road to *Philadelphia*. I had almost forgot to speak something of the Quakers yearly Meetings, which I should have done in my Description of *Philadelphia*, or *Burlington*. They meet yearly at one of these Places alternately, by Agreement, when all Sorts of the best Provisions are provided for the Reception of great Numbers of the Brethren assembled from all Quarters, who are sometimes so numerous, that there is not room for them; which obliges them to disperse into the adjacent Villages for Quarter, but return in the Day to the Town.

At these times they dispense their Charity to the Poor and Needy, without any regard to particular Sect or Party: I have partaken of their Benevolence. Their stay is from *Saturday* Night, when they first arrive, till about *Wednesday*; when they reward the Servants where they reside liberally, and usually leave Money in the Family, for the Use of the

Poor, which is given at their Discretion. These Meetings are for the rebuking of Schisms, that sometimes arise among them; and to inquire into the external Behaviour of the Professors, and to preserve Unanimity. In a word, they shew to Mankind, that they are strict Observe[r]s of good Nature and Hospitality, and keep up to the due Observance of the Evangelical Precepts, and the Moral Law.

My Master employed me in his Business: I continued satisfied with him for sometime; but being desirous to settle at *Philadelphia*, during the rest of my Servitude, I declared to him, I would stay no longer, and desired him to dispose of me to some other Master, and insisted upon it, agreeably to the Tenour of my Indenture. This Demand made him cross to me, and I attempted an Escape, but was taken, and put into Prison; but was soon released, with a promise to satisfy my Demand. About a Fortnight after, we went to the Mayor of *Philadelphia*, his Name was *Griffith*,[4] a Man of exact Justice, tho' an *Irishman*, who reconciled us; so I returned back to *Burlington*, and continued with him three Years, he forgiving me the other Two: I was ever after perfectly pleased with my Master's Behaviour to me, which was generous.

There lived in the Family a Relation of his, named *Hannah Lambert*, a Gentlewoman of Beauty, good Parts, and a good Fortune, Daughter to Mr *Thomas Lambert*, a Native of *Yorkshire*.[5] One Day as this Lady and myself was crossing [the] *Delaware*, in a Canoe, it overset; so being in Danger, I forgot my own for her Safety, and taking her round the Small of the Waist, with one Arm, swam by the help of the other to the other Side of the River. She so sensibly remembered this Service, that all the Time of my stay in this Family, I never wanted Money. Her Father gave me five Pounds, and when ever I went into the Country, I generally made his House my resting Place, where I was very civily treated.

Our Family consisted of a Wife and two Daughters, with a Nephew, a Negro Slave, a bought Servant,[6] and myself, with the aforesaid Gen-

4. Thomas Griffitts served as Philadelphia's mayor from October 7, 1729, to October 6, 1731, and from October 2, 1733, to October 1, 1734.

5. Thomas Lambert arrived from Yorkshire, England, on the ship *Shield* in 1678 and resided in Nottingham Township, New Jersey (W.J.P. [*sic*], "Major-General John Lambert," in "Notes and Queries," *PMHB* 12 [1888]: 191). He died in 1733, according to a report in the *American Weekly Mercury*, March 20–27, 1733. When Hannah Lambert married Dr. Thomas Cadwalader in 1738, her wealth enticed him to give up his Philadelphia practice, move to her residence in Trenton, and take over the administration of her very valuable estate; they subsequently had seven children (William Henry Rawle, "Col. Lambert Cadwalader: A Sketch," *PMHB* 10 [1886]: 2–3).

6. The "bought Servant" was Aaron Middleton (see Figure 17).

tlewoman. We had a next Door Neighbour, called *William Cullum,*[7] a *Lincolnshire* Man, and a Baker: He came to us one Day, as my master and myself were making Nails for a Bellows for a Forge; and laying down upon the Bellows Board Three-pence and Sugar, writ the following Words in Chalk, and left the Place, we not knowing from whence the money came.

Here's Money, Sugar, fetch some Rum,
And when the Liquors made, I come.

My Master perceiving it, said, Well, this is *William Cullum's,* in order to shew his Wit, and order'd me to answer it Extempore. I first fetched the Rum, then made the Liquor, which was *Bombo,* and writ under the foregoing Lines.

The Liquor's made, besure to come,
Or send more Sugar, and more Rum.

Which my Friend perceived, laughed, and gave me a Shilling, with which I merrily quaffed.

One Night as I was in Bed with my Fellow Servant, being awake, the Chamber Door opened without any Noise, and I perceiv'd something coming cross the Floor, like a Ghost, in White, with a black Face. The Sight was so terrifying, that I shrunk under the Bed Cloaths, and sweated heartily, and endeavoured to wake my Friend, but to no Purpose. It came to the Bedside, and stooping, grined, and stared me in the Face, and beckened with its Hand: At which I shiver'd so much, and my Chops chatter'd, as if beating a March; but recollecting myself, I demanded of it what it wanted. Then it beckoned again, and left the Room; but soon after came again, looked earnestly at me. When I said, *Lord! why do you come here?* It answer'd, *Nothing with you,* as I well remember, and then went away, the Door shooting after it, without any Noise. I was very positive it was a Spirit, and told the Family the next Morning; who said, it was a Negro killed some Years since by her Master, and that they had often seen it.[8]

The [Delaware] River is supposed to have its Rise from a Lake, in the

7. A baker in Burlington, William Collum died in 1740 or 1741, leaving his property to his wife, Mary. Isaac Pearson's will in 1748 mentioned Mary Collum as a neighbor living on High Street. (Wills, 2:105, 373.)

8. See Appendix G for the 1686 case of the murder of a slave in Moraley's residence in Burlington.

Mountains of *Canada*, and is believed from its first Spring to the *Capes*, in its Windings, to be above 2000 Miles in length.[9] In the Heat of Summer, nothing affords a more pleasant and delightful Prospect than it does. On both Sides are to be seen handsome Houses, surrounded with great Numbers of Gardens and Orchards, blessed with great Variety of Fruits, salutiferious Plants and Herbs. Along the Banks are found divers Sorts of curious Shells, which are carefully gather'd and sent as Rareties to *Europe*. Great Numbers of large Sturgeon gamble on the Water, often times leaping quite out. The Boys in a Summer's Evening swim, but keep near the Shore, for fear of the Sharks. The Navigation extends above 200 Miles; but at a Town called *Trent Town*, twenty Miles from *Philadelphia*, no Ship or Boat can pass, by reason of a Chain of Rocks cross the River from Side to Side.[10]

In the Month of *July*, in 1731, one *Lawrence Houlton*,[11] and myself, being Fishing in a Canoe, a Water Snake, of about six Foot long, offer'd to board us: We had much ado to prevent him. He jumped several Times, but we beat him of[f] with our Fishing Sticks. About half an Hour after, we discover'd a bald Eagle, hovering in the Air, who descended often, and at last seized a lame wild Goose, swimming on the Water, and carried it off. These Birds live chiefly upon Fish, and on that Account are generally found near the Rivers; they often have Battles in the Air with the Hawks, but are always beaten.

Along the Banks of this River are many trading Towns, with convenient Docks and Keys, where are landed Goods, for the mutual support of each other, such as Wood for Firing, Rum, Sugar, Molasses; likewise coarse Linen, of which there are some small Manufactures, tolerably good. Fish is so plentiful, I have seen large Boats and Barges, loaden to the Brim with them, such as Roach,[12] Pearch, and Trouts, larger than those caught in *England*.

9. The Delaware River actually originates in the Catskill Mountains of New York and runs about 370 miles to the Delaware Bay. The bay extends for an additional 50 miles before emptying into the Atlantic Ocean.

10. Trenton is 116 nautical miles, and Philadelphia 80 nautical miles, from the Atlantic Ocean by way of the Delaware Bay and River.

11. Lawrence Houlton (Holstin, Holstein, Holson, or Holston) lived in Pilesgrove, Salem County, New Jersey, from at least 1715 until his death in 1750. He was not a wealthy man; his personal estate was valued at less than £9 at his death. (AIS; Wills, 2:244.)

12. According to Samuel Johnson, "a *roach* is a fish of no great reputation for his dainty taste: his spawn is accounted much better than any other part of him: he is accounted the water sheep, for his simplicity and foolishness; and it is noted, that *roaches* recover strength, and grow in a fortnight after spawning" (*Johnson's Dictionary*, 348).

On both Sides are many Creeks, as large as most of our Rivers, which being Navigable for small Vessels, are made use of to convey Necessaries to the Country People, from the larger and remote Country Towns. These Creeks are so deep, that no Bridges are to be met with to cross over, so Boats and Ferries are provided at certain Stages. The People generally chuse to live near these Creeks, which is the Reason the Country far from them is thinly inhabited.

In the midst of the River *Delaware*, are many small Islands, some of them two Miles in length, others half the length, which are fertile. In the Summer the Cows will swim to them, from either Shore, and graze till the Evening, when they will return, but sometimes with the Loss of a Leg, by the Shirks. I have been in some of these Islands. Here is one call'd *Perriwig Island*,[13] from its resembling one in its Shape: It is two Miles and a Half long, and lies seventeen Miles from *Burlington*, nothing has a more Romantick look than this Place: It is furnished with many Sorts of Fruits and Roots, especially wild Grapes, and of the Muskadel Kind, with Sassafras.

Caves are here so convenient, as if perfected by Art: in one of them the Bones of a Man were found, which if all the Rest were in the same Proportion, would form a Skelliton of near thirty Feet in length. I saw a Thigh Bone and a Tooth, which last would, in the Hollow of it, contain near half a Pint of any Liquid.

Farther up the Country are Copper Mines, producing Copper near as good as that of *Sweden*, which much inriches the Proprietors, and imploys great numbers.[14] Coal Mines have been discovered; but as Wood is Cheaper, it is not used. In many places are to be seen the remains of *Deucalion's*,[15] or *Noah's* Flood; such as the Figures of Fishes imprinted upon divers Sorts of Shells, with several Strata's of Earth; some with Shells, others with the Bones of Animals. Near *New York*, Cottages have been discovered buried under Ground above two hundred Feet deep.

I have inquired of the *Indians*, if they had any Account of Time

13. Shaped something like a periwig (a wig), Newbold Island is somewhat smaller than Moraley indicates, and it lies about seven miles upstream from the town of Burlington. Facing the island on the western shore of the river was Pennsbury.

14. In 1749 Peter Kalm noted the earlier economic importance of these New Jersey copper mines, although they had flooded by the time Kalm traveled through the area (Kalm, *America of 1750*, 2:621). The history of these Bergen County copper mines is in Wayne Bodle, "'Such a Noise in the World': Schuyler's Mine and the Response in the Middle Colonies, 1719–1729" (Paper presented at the Seminar of the Transformation of Philadelphia Project, University of Pennsylvania, March 20, 1989).

15. According to Greek mythology, Deucalion and his wife Pyrrha were the sole survivors of a flood sent by Zeus to destroy the human race.

among them, in order to trace out a History, to give Mankind some Account of their Origine; but they assured me, they have no written Tradition, nor any Memorial left them by their Forefathers, that can give the least Satisfaction.

From the frequent discovery of human Bones, of such Magnitude as are continually found, we may reasonably believe Men were formerly of larger Stature than at present; and to make this appear the more probable, there have been discovered proportionable Caves for their Reception, above two hundred Feet under Ground; which makes it plain, that the Race of large Men ended by the universal Flood: This Opinion is believed by the *English* here, with whom I have discoursed concerning these Matters.[16]

16. Colonial Americans commonly attributed large fossil bones to an earlier race of giant human beings. See David Levin, "Giants in the Earth: Science and the Occult in Cotton Mather's Letters to the Royal Society," *William and Mary Quarterly*, 3rd ser., 45 (1988): 751–70.

6 PLANTATIONS IN PENNSYLVANIA—INDIAN CORN—"THE BEST POOR MAN'S COUNTRY IN THE WORLD"—WILD BEASTS—RATTLE SNAKES—HORN SNAKES—HUMMING BIRDS—LOCUSTS—BUTTERFLIES—THE NEGROES—SLAVE LAWS—BOUGHT SERVANTS.

EFORE I observed, that I continued with my Master at *Burlington*, in perfect Concord. I acting as a Watchmaker, he often detached me into the Country to clean Clocks and Watches: It was in these Journeys I had an Opportunity of discovering what I have observed relating to the several Descriptions contained in this Book.

Almost every inhabitant, in the Country, have a Plantation, some two or more; there being no Land lett as in *England*,[1] where Gentlemen live on the Labour of the Farmer, to whom he grants a short Lease, which expiring, he is either raised in his Rent, or discharged his Farm. Here they improve their Lands themselves, with the Assistance both of bought Servants and Negroes. They raise *Indian* Corn, for the Subsis-

1. Although land ownership was more prevalent in the Middle Colonies than in England, Moraley's claim that land was not leased in the Mid-Atlantic region was certainly exaggerated. See, e.g., Lucy Simler, "The Landless Worker: An Index of Economic and Social Change in Chester County, Pennsylvania, 1750–1820," *PMHB* 114 (1990): 163–200.

tence of their Families, after this Method: The Ears of Corn of the last Years growth is sown in the Beginning of *April*; they dig a Trench in the Ground, about five Inches deep, into which they strew the Grains, a few at a Time, for fear they should Sprout out too thick, and cover them lightly with Earth. After six Weeks it shoots out, then the Planters rake with a Hough the Ground, round the Stalk, to strengthen it: This is done every six Weeks, till the Corn is confirmed, which is brought to perfection the Beginning of *September*, when they strip the Corn from the Stalks, which they convey to their Granaries, leaving the Stalks to rot, which fertilizes their Land. With this Corn they make a kind of hasty Pudding, boiling it in Salt and Water, till it is thick; then pour it into a Dish, and serve it up with Milk, sometimes with Butter, but most commonly with Treacle.[2] It is a hungry Food, and is called *Mush*, being not unlike a Dish called *Cous Cous*, used in the Kingdoms of *Fez* and *Morocco*. They make use of it for Puddings, both boiled and baked, which with Eggs, is as good as a Rice Pudding. Raisins and Currants are seldom used, by reason of their Dearness, being Twelve-pence a Pound.

This Country produces not only almost every Fruit, Herb, and Root, as grows in *Great Britain*, but divers Sorts unknown to us. Bread Corn is superior to ours for Whiteness, and Cheaper. Barley is not so good, tho' they make Beer of it: Our Ten Shilling Small Beer is infinitely preferrable to any brewed there. Butter is very good, but Eight-pence a Pound; so Fish is generally eaten with the Butter it is fried in, with a little Vinegar to make it sharp. Butchers Meat, particularly Pork, is cheaper and better than with us; being fed with *Indian* Corn and Acrons. I have seen the Planters shake the Peach Trees to the Hogs.[3]

The Country is every where diversify'd with Woods, and well manured Farms: And the hospitable Inhabitants dispence their Favours to the Traveller, the Poor and Needy. I have travelled some Hundreds of Miles at no Expense, Meat and Drink being bestowed upon all the subjects of *Great Britain*; for they strive to out-do one another in Works

2. Commonly eaten in England, treacle is a syrup produced during the refining of sugar.

3. Casting peaches before swine was one of the wonders of the Delaware Valley, and many visitors remarked on the incredible natural abundance implied by this practice. See, e.g., the comment made by Gabriel Thomas in 1689 in Albert Cook Myers, ed., *Narratives of Early Pennsylvania, West New Jersey, and Delaware, 1630–1707* (New York: Barnes & Noble, 1912), 324. And Peter Kalm noted that in Europe "hardly any people but the rich" could eat peaches, while in the middle colonies they were fodder for pigs (Kalm, *America of 1750*, 1:40–41).

of good Nature and Charity. In short, it is the best poor Man's Country in the World; and, I believe, if this was sufficiently known by the miserable Objects we have in our Streets, Multitudes would be induced to go thither. Journeymens Wages are Five Shillings a Day,[4] and is paid to Joiners, Carpenters, Bricklayers, and Barbers, &c.

The Rivers are well stored with Fish, as Roaches, Pearch, Trout, Cat Fish, which makes excellent Broth. Sturgeon I have bought one eight Foot long for Ten-pence; Flounders, Eels, Sun-Fish, Rock-Fish, better than our Cod; Oysters larger than *English* ones, and much better, the Shells are one Foot long. Here are Swans, Peacocks, Geese, Turkies, Ducks, Pidgeons, both Wild and Tame; Cocks and Hens are cheap, a fat Hen is sold for Two-pence Half-penny in the Markets; Pheasants, Partridges, Woodcocks, Quails, Plover, Snipes, besides small Birds unknown to us.

Here are Rabbits, but they are rather Hares, smaller than ours, they are seldom larger than *English* Rabbits, and the Flesh tasting like the Flesh of *English* Hares. Squirrels are of different Kinds, the smallest having Wings like a Bat, which helps them to fly from Tree to Tree. Panthers, Wolves, and Bears, are common; besides Horses, the hardiest in the World, for after a Riding of many Miles, being hot, they leave them standing in the Streets all Night, without catching Cold.

Otters, Badgers, Wild Cats, and a Beast called Scunck, who if you approach near them, will piss on their Tails, and switch them in your Face, and the Stink will continue above a Week. The Possum, which will retire to a tree when pursued, where hanging by its Tail, which it twists round the Branches, will defend itself against its Enemies, with the young in its Belly, which is a false one, for that use.

Here are Foxes, both Red, Grey, and White; besides Racoons, of the same Nature and Qualities, of whose Furs, worked up with Beaver, are made the best of Hats. Frogs are numerous, and of different Colours; their Legs are much longer than those of *Europe*; some are coloured like a Leopard, others streak'd like a Tyger with black and yellow Spots, which makes them of a frightful appearance. Here are no Toads; Lizards are of various Sorts and Colours, but not Poisonous; and are looked upon as Forerunners of Snakes, which are of many Sorts; as First,

The Rattle Snake, about six or seven Feet in Length, and so Poisonous, that if the Party bitten, does not cut off the Part bit, Death immediately ensues. The Natives have found out a Plant, which, if

4. Master craftsmen hired journeymen on a daily, weekly, or often longer basis.

presently applied to the Wound, perfects a Cure. The Discovery was made by the Indians thus; when a Snake has bitten either Man or Beast, he presently flies to seek out this Plant, and eats some of it, to prevent its poisoning its self; and it has been discover'd, when he has missed of this Plant, he has been found Dead: the Truth of this has been confirmed to me by several discreet Persons.

The Rattles do not begin to grow till the Snake is three Years old, then every Year one is produced: Whenever this Animal leaps at either Man or Beast, he first shakes his Tail, then rises half his Length. This seems to be a Contrivance of the good Providence of God, in order to prevent the direful Consequences from the bite of this noxious Creature. One *Joseph Rose*,[5] of *New Jersey*, shewed me a Set of Rattles, to the Number of 37 from one Snake; so the Age of it was 40 Years.[6]

The Horn Snake is the next Dangerous, about the same Length and Bigness, having a Horn at the Extremity of its Tail, through which there is a Concavity, where with he ejects his Poison. If by accident he strikes his Horn into a Tree, it dies in two Days time, and the Leaves wither, and fall to the Ground. This I thought incredible, but the Natives attested it to me for Truth; and is not to be wonder'd at, considering all Trees and Plants have contain'd in them a vegetable Life.

The Red Belly'd Snake is commonly in Length five or six Feet, he is very Poisonous. The Green Snake of the same Length and Qualities. The Water Snake large, and extreme hurtful. The Garter Snake harmless and beautiful. The Yellow or Wampum Snake, as hurtful as any. Two Sorts of Adders, or Vipers, hurtful, as large again as ours. Two Sorts of Black Snakes, so bold in Gendering time, that they will run after People and bite them, but not Venomous; they are six, seven, or eight Foot long.[7]

5. Two men named Joseph Rose appear in the surviving records. One was the Philadelphia printer who assumed the business of his father after his death in 1738 (*American Weekly Mercury*, June 28—July 4, 1738). Another Joseph Rose (1704–76) was born in Ireland and migrated to Philadelphia, arriving in the city on October 21, 1729. He moved to Burlington, where he eventually married a wealthy widow and then moved to Lancaster, Pennsylvania. He was admitted to the bar in 1750. See Charles I. Landis, "The Juliana Library Company in Lancaster," *PMHB* 43 (1919): 243.

6. Moraley's accounts of snakes are better read as local folk belief than as a naturalist's observations. Many of the superstitions and tall tales recounted by Moraley survived into the twentieth century. See Phares H. Hertzog, "Snakes and Snakelore of Pennsylvania," *Pennsylvania Folklife* 17 (1967): 14–17.

7. Peter Kalm also noted the excessive numbers, length, and aggressiveness of black snakes in the countryside surrounding Philadelphia (Kalm, *America of 1750*, 1:313–17).

Lastly Ground Snakes, about seven or eight Inches long, like our Hag Worms.

These Animals in the Summer time frequent the Woods, which not being much resorted to by Men, they increase in such Abundance, that I believe, where we have One, here are five Thousand; one shall often meet them sunning themselves, and in the Woods concealed under old rotten Wood, and dried Leaves, where they have a secure Retreat. If any accident befalls them, by being wounded, they live till the setting of the Sun, then die. They subsist upon Frogs, and it is diverting to see the fear the Frog is under at the approach of his Adversary. The Snake pursuing, and the Frog leaping from him, till finding it in Vain to resist his superior Enemy, leaps into his Jaws, who is sometime in Swallowing him, always beginning at his Legs.

The Humming Bird is very remarkable for his Smallness and Beauty; his Body no larger than a Bee. He is so called for his Humming when he flies. His Bill is long and straight, in Proportion, as a Woodcock's. His Body beautifully adorned with Variety of Feathers of different Colours, Gold being the most perspicuous, and so fine, one would think they were Down. He never alights on the Ground, but hovers, in the Summer time, over the mellifluous Flowers, his proper Food; when, by the Help of his Bill, he sucks out the Sweets, and retires to the Cherry Tree, his natural abode, where he builds his Nest.

I have observed a Wasp to build his Nest over a Smith's Chimney, in a very odd Manner. I was working at the Forge, when I espied a small Chimney raised against the Wall of the Forge, near the Fire. It was about six Inches long, made of wet Dirt, which the Animal brought in its Mouth, about the Bigness of a Pea, and with its Feet plaster'd against the Wall, beginning from the Bottom; and had first made a Convex, in order to support the System, like an arched Door-way, or Window, and raised the whole Fabrick in a Convex Form: At the Upper-end he laid his Nest.

Here is a Beetle, called by the Natives a Tumbleturd, which for the Oddness of its Building its Nest, deserves a Description. About *April*, both Male and Female, leave their old abiding Place, to find a more proper one; which having done, find out a Hole about two Foot under Ground, into which they descend, by a Crack made by the Heat of the Sun, in order to make their Nest, then they leave the Place, and after they have found a small Piece of wet Earth, the Bigness of a Pea, they roll it along the Ground, it growing as it gathers the Dust, to the Place appointed, where they tumble it in, and lay their Eggs in the midst of the Ball, which is as large as a Coit,[8] where they are hatched by the Sun.

The Manner of rolling the Ball is thus: The Male sets his fore Feet against the Ball, and drives it forward. On the opposite Side the Female stands erect and with her fore Feet pulls it towards her. When either of them are tired, they do not forsake their Work, but change their Posts. Sometimes one of them being very weary with shoving with its Fore Legs, reverses itself, and standing upon its Fore Legs, shoves the Ball with its Hind Legs, the Head being downwards. If by any Accident one of them should be missing, the other does the whole Duty, by driving the Ball alone.

I have often, in observing these Creatures, reflected on the wonderful Effects of Nature, and admired the Infinite Wisdom of the Creator, who has embued the least of his Productions with a seeming Degree of Reason (if I may be allowed to term it so) in order to bring about his Divine Purposes. In this Part of the World, one has always an Opportunity of observing such a diversity of Wonders, as naturally raises in us a Co[n]templation of the abundant Goodness, Power and Mercy, of the Beneficent Creator.

The Mocking Bird, is another Animal, of an odd Nature: He is called so for his incessant Noise like the Barking of a Dog, and often occasions the unwary Traveller, to mistake his Way. I was once lost in the Woods by hearing one of them, and tracing out the Noise; sometimes it was before me, then behind, that I was five Hours before I could find the Way home.

About the same time appears another Bird call'd *Whip for Will*, from his Cry, being like the Expression of those Words: He usually begins to tune his Pipe about Nine in the Morning, sitting on a Branch of a Tree, not far from the Ground, and continues till the Setting of the Sun.

Here are Bald Eagles, having no Feathers, on their Heads: They hover over Rivers, and very frequently catch Fish, by suddenly darting on the Water. Here are also Hawks and Vultures, but for Linnets, Green Birds, Larks, Goldfinches, Bulfinches, and Chaffinches, here are none to be found. Bees are numerous, who leave their Honey in hollow Trees. Several People make a Living by seeking for it; and so plenty, that one

8. A Coit, or quoit, is a flattish ring of iron. In the eighteenth-century game of the same name, it was thrown at a pin stuck in the ground with the object of encircling the pin.

Hundred Pound Weight has been found in one Tree. Musketoes are troublesome in the Summer time; but the People make Fires before their Houses in the Evenings, which banishes them away.

Before I left *America* there was such a prodigious Flight of Pidgeons seen that almost darkened the Air, and infested the Fields and Villages, and so tame, that they became the Food of the Inhabitants for a Month together. They alighted in whole Flocks, and rested upon the Tops of Houses and Barns in a starving Condition, being by Necessity drove from some other Country. In 1732, in *July* and *September* an Insect called a Locust appeared, which was looked upon as a bad Omen, and it accordingly happened, for presently after, they came in such Swarms, that the Trees were covered with them, and devour'd the Leaves and Fruit: Their Bodies are about the bigness of the Humming Bird, having a black Head, and Eyes jutting out like black Beads. Their Colour is not unlike a Spanish Fly. About seven Years before this, a Swarm of Squirrels came over [the] *Delaware* River, and entered the Houses.

Here are Many Sorts of Butterflies, larger than those in *England*, so finely coloured, as causes in the Beholder both Wonder and Delight: They build their Nests in the Leaves of Cabbages, and continue their Abode in them, till their Young are brought to Perfection, then leave them to shift for themselves. So admirable are the Effects of the Divine Providence in supporting the most minute of his Productions, that makes me break out in the Words of *David, How manifold, O Lord! are all thy Works; in Wisdom hast thou created them.*[9]

At the first Peopling [of] these Colonies, there was a Necessity of employing a great Number of Hands, for the clearing the Land, being over-grown with Wood for some Hundred of Miles; to which Intent, the first Settlers not being sufficient of themselves to improve those Lands, were not only obliged to purchase a great Number of *English* Servants to assist them, to whom they granted great Immunities, and at the Expiration of their Servitude, Land was given to encourage them to continue there; but were likewise obliged to purchase Multitudes of Negro Slaves from *Africa*, by which Means they are become the richest Farmers in the World, paying no Rent, nor giving Wages either to purchased Servants or Negro Slaves; so that instead of finding the Planter Rack-rented, as the *English* Farmer, you will taste of their Liberality, they living in Affluence and Plenty.

9. Psalms 104:24: "O Lord, how manifold are thy works! in wisdom hast thou made them all: the earth is full of thy riches."

Juſt Imported and to be *Sold*,
By *Robert Ellis* and *John Ryan*
A PARCEL of fine young Healthy, Negroe Slaves, Boys and Girls, and are to be Sold very reaſonable. They may be ſeen at ſaid *Ellis*'s Houſe in *Water ſtreet*.
N. B. Three or four Months Credit will be given on good Security, or an abatement of *Twenty Shillings* made in each Slave on preſent Payment.

Figure 15. Newspaper advertisement of slaves for sale, *American Weekly Mercury* (Philadelphia), June 8–15, 1738.

The Condition of the Negroes is very bad, by reason of the Severity of the Laws, there being no Laws made in Favour of these unhap[p]y Wretches: For the least Trespass, they undergo the severest Punishment; but their Masters make them some amends, by suffering them to marry, which makes them easier, and often prevents their running away. The Consequence of their marrying is this, all their Posterity are Slaves without Redemption; and it is in vain to attempt an Escape, tho' they often endeavour it; for the Laws against them are so severe, that being caught after running away, they are unmercifully whipped; and if they die under the Discipline, their Masters suffer no Punishment, there being no Law against murdering them.[10] So if one Man kills another's Slave, he is only obliged to pay his Value to the Master, besides Damages that may accrue for the Loss of him in his Business.

The Masters generally allow them a Piece of Ground, with Materials for improving it. The Time of working for themselves, is *Sundays*, when

10. New Jersey's slave law of 1716 required citizens to whip both slaves coming into the colony without permission and resident bondspeople discovered five miles from their master's home without a written pass. Courts could order unlimited corporal punishment of slaves who attacked people "possessing Christianity"—that is, whites. See James C. Connolly, "Slavery in Colonial New Jersey and the Causes Operating Against Its Extension," *Proceedings of the New Jersey Historical Society* 14 (1929): 194–99.

Figure 16. Runaway slave, 1730. William Moore of Chester County, Pennsylvania, described his fugitive slave, Jack, as wearing "a new ozenburg Shirt, a pair of strip'd home-spun Breeches, a strip'd ticking Wastecoat, an old dimity Coat of his Master's with Buttons of Horse teeth set in Brass, and Cloth Sleeves, a felt Hat almost new."

they raise on their own Account divers Sorts of Corn and Grain, and sell it in the Markets. They buy with the Money Cloaths for themselves and Wives; as for the Children, they belong to the Wives Master, who bring them up; so the Negro need fear no Expense, his Business being to get them for his Master's use, who is as tender of them as his own Children. On *Sundays* in the evening they converse with their Wives, and drink Rum, or Bumbo, and smoak Tobacco, and the next Morning return to their Master's Labour.

They are seldom made free, for fear of being burthensome to the Provinces, there being a Law, that no Master shall manumise them, unless he gives Security they shall not be thrown upon the Province, by settling Land on them for their Support.[11]

11. Masters were legally obligated to post a bond of £200 when manumitting a slave, and they could be required to support their former bondspeople if they became a burden on the community. Such

Their Marriages are diverting; for when the Day is appointed for the Solemnization, Notice is given to all the Negroes and their Wives to be ready. The Masters of the new Couple provide handsomely for the Entertainment of the Company. The Inhabitants generally grace the Nuptials with their Presence, when all Sorts of the best Provisions are to be met with. They chuse some *Englishman* to read the Marriage Ceremony out of the Common Prayer Book; after which they sing and dance and drink till they get drunk. Then a Negro goes about the Company and collects Money for the Use of the Person who marry'd them, which is laid out in a Handkerchief, and presented to him.

This is the only free Day they have, except Sundays, throughout the whole Course of their Lives, for then they banish from them all Thoughts of the Wretchedness of their Condition. The Day being over, they return to their Slavery. I have often heard them say, they did not think God made them Slaves, any more than other Men, and wondered that Christians, especially *Englishmen*, should use them so barbarously. But there is a Necessity of using them hardly, being of an obdurate, stubborn Disposition; and when they have it in their Power to rebel, are extremely cruel.[12]

The Condition of bought Servants is very hard, notwithstanding their indentures are made in *England*, wherein it is expressly stipulated, that they shall have, at their Arrival, all the Necessaries specified in those Indentures, to be given 'em by their future Masters, such as Clothes, Meat, and Drink; yet upon Complaint made to a Magistrate against the Master for Nonperformance, the Master is generally heard before the Servant, and it is ten to one if he does not get his Licks for his Pains, as I have experienced upon the like Occassion, to my Cost.

If they endeavor to escape, which is next to impossible, there being a Reward for taking up any Person who travels without a Pass, which is extended all over the *British* Colonies, their Masters immediately issue

---

laws naturally discouraged the manumission of slaves. Free African Americans in New Jersey were subject to a variety of social and legal restrictions—for example, they could have only a life interest in property rather than own it in fee simple, and therefore they could not leave real estate to their families because it escheated to the Crown on their death. See Connolly, "Slavery in Colonial New Jersey," 194–99.

12. Moraley may have heard about the first major organized slave revolt in British North America, which occurred in New York in 1712; authorities put eighteen slaves to death after the revolt. See Kenneth Scott, "The Slave Insurrection in New York in 1712," *New-York Historical Quarterly* 45 (1961): 43–74; and J. Davis, *A Rumor of Revolt: The Great Negro Plot in Colonial New York* (New York: Pantheon, 1985).

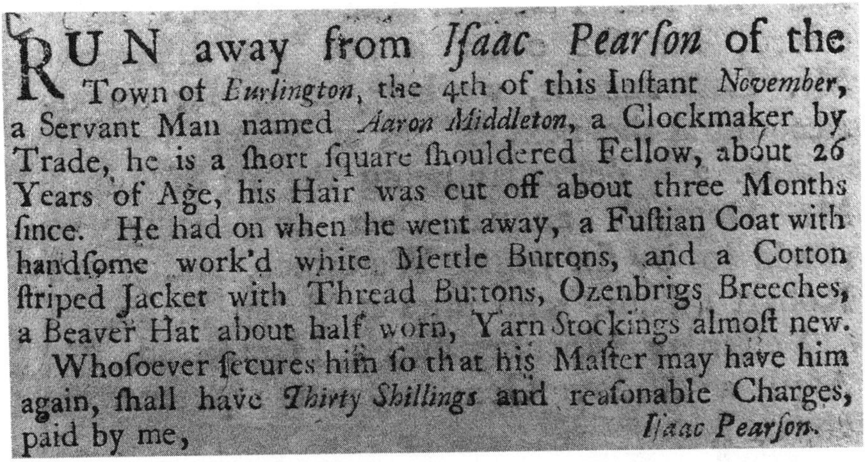

RUN away from *Iſaac Pearſon* of the Town of *Burlington*, the 4th of this Inſtant *November*, a Servant Man named *Aaron Middleton*, a Clockmaker by Trade, he is a ſhort ſquare ſhouldered Fellow, about 26 Years of Age, his Hair was cut off about three Months ſince. He had on when he went away, a Fuſtian Coat with handſome work'd white Mettle Buttons, and a Cotton ſtriped Jacket with Thread Buttons, Ozenbrigs Breeches, a Beaver Hat about half worn, Yarn Stockings almoſt new.
Whoſoever ſecures him ſo that his Maſter may have him again, ſhall have *Thirty Shillings* and reaſonable Charges, paid by me, *Iſaac Pearſon*.

Figure 17. Newspaper advertisement for runaway servant of Isaac Pearson, *American Weekly Mercury* (Philadelphia), November 2–9, 1732.

out a Reward for the apprehending them, from Thirty Shillings to Five Pound, as they think proper, and this generally brings them back again. Printed and Written Advertisements are also set up against the Trees and publick Places in the Town, besides those in the News-papers. Notwithstanding these Difficulties, they are perpetually running away, but seldom escape; for a hot Pursuit being made, brings them back, when a Justice settles the Expences, and the Servant is oblig'd to serve a longer time.[13]

13. By New Jersey law, escaped servants were to serve two extra days for each day they were absent, and the courts could add additional time to compensate masters for expenses incurred in capturing runaways (Abbot Emerson Smith, *Colonists in Bondage: White Servitude and Convict Labor in America, 1607–1776* [Chapel Hill: University of North Carolina Press, 1947], 267). Figure 17 reproduces a newspaper advertisement for a servant who absconded from Moraley's master.

7 THE INDIANS IN PENNSYLVANIA—THEIR HABITS, MANNERS, AND RELIGION—COLONIAL CURRENCY—THE GOVERNOR AND HIS COUNCIL—THE FAMILY OF WILLIAM PENN—CHARITY OF THE QUAKERS—DRINKS—FISH AND FRUIT—THE CLIMATE—"THE TENNIS BALL OF FORTUNE."

HE Native Inhabitants are the *Indians*, who are a civiliz'd, handsome-limb'd People: None amongst them were ever born deform'd or crook'd.[1] Their Complexion is of a Copper Colour; with broad flat Faces, thick Lips and Noses. The Men are generally tall and slender, but the Women are short and fat. Their Habit, both Men and Women, is much alike, since their Acquaintance with the *English*, most of them wearing a Match Coat, made of coarse *Scotch* Plaid, the Breeches and Stockings of

1. The Europeans called the people living along the Delaware Bay by the name of "Delaware." These Unami-speaking people, more correctly called the Lenape, inhabited what is now New Jersey and parts of Pennsylvania, Delaware, and New York. Of course, Moraley's description of their health is exaggerated. His views are in accord with the somewhat romanticized notions adopted by many Europeans as the Native American population declined along the eastern seaboard and no longer posed a substantial threat to the white invaders. See Herbert C. Kraft, *The Lenape: Archaeology, History, and Ethnography* (Newark: New Jersey Historical Society, 1986), xvii–xviii; and Peter O. Wacker, *Land and People: A Cultural Geography of Preindustrial New Jersey: Origins and Settlement Patterns* (New Brunswick, N.J.: Rutgers University Press, 1975), 57–60, 104–5.

the same, with Cotton stuff'd in their Ears, and Brass Thimbles hanging at them. But the Kings have Belts of Wampum, which is their Money, hanging about their Necks.[2]

They hunt Deer for their Living, and other Kinds of Beasts, both wild and tame.[3] The King[4] first receive[s] his Tribute out of the Profits arising from their hunting, then they sell the Remainder to the *English* for Sugar, Molasses, Guns, Gun-powder, and Rum. With the last they make themselves drunk; and when all is spent, return home. I have met them in the Fields in their Return, sitting in a Ring, so drunk, that they could not stir from the Place.

In the Succession of their Kings they observe an Hereditary Right, the Son always taking his Father's Place. These People pay them a Respect suitable to their Dignity; though their Grandeur is not much superior to that of their Subjects, only differing from them in living idle, and upon their Tribute, which is not very great. Their Dominions are not above forty Miles in Circumference, wherein are no Towns, but dispers'd Wigwams, or low Houses.

There is always a perfect Agreement subsists between the *English* and them, for generally every two Years, or three at furthest, they visit the Governors of the Provinces, attended by near two thousand of their Subjects, in order to renew the ancient Friendship between them.[5] As soon as Notice is given of their Approach, the Governor sets out to meet them, attended by the principal Inhabitants, and pays them extraordinary Honours, treating them and their Followers several Days together. After this they enter into Treaty with one another, which is either to ratify and confirm the ancient Ones, or make new Ones. Then they return Home, loaded with Presents and Drink.

They are so just in the due Observance of these Treaties that there is not one Instance of Breach of Covenant can be brought against them.

2. Wampum consisted of cylindrical beads made from the ends of polished shells threaded on strings; these served as the currency among many Native Americans and in their early dealings with Europeans (Kraft, *The Lenape*, 202–7).

3. Most Lenape engaged in a mixed economy, depending on agriculture, hunting, gathering, and fishing for their livelihood. By 1730 some Lenape were able to carry on their traditional way of life, although others in the area grew increasingly dependent on agriculture as hunting became less viable. See ibid., 225; Wacker, *Land and People*, 60–68.

4. A chief, usually referred to as a "king" or "sachem" by Europeans, headed each Lenape band and exercised considerable influence although not unlimited power (Wacker, *Land and People*, 58).

5. Although the Quakers in West Jersey generally lived peacefully with the Lenape, Moraley overstates the harmony between the races. By 1730 relatively few Lenape still lived in the area, which clearly helped minimize conflict. (Ibid., 84–88.)

These Agreements are chiefly relating to Violences that have or may be committed by the Subjects on either Side; and if a Murder is committed by an *Indian* upon an *English* Subject, they will send out Parties and pursue the Murderer till they have found him, and then deliver up the Offender to Justice. But if an *Englishman* Murder an *Indian*, and the *English* refuse to deliver him up to Justice, they will come in great Bodies and demand him, to be punish'd by them. But of late it is agreed to punish each Offender where they find him; so if the *Indians* find a Subject of *England* guilty of Murder, they punish him with Death, though the Offence was committed against an *Englishman*. In the same Manner the *English* proceed against an *Indian*; by which means all Acts of Hostility are prevented.

As to their notions of Religion, they are very wild, having none establish'd among them; but believe there is a God, Creator of all Things, endowed with Wisdom, Goodness, and Mercy; and believe they shall be judged, punished, and rewarded, according as they observe the moral Precepts instilled into them by the Light of Nature, and the Tradition of their Fathers.[6]

Their Arms for War were formerly Bows and Arrows; but since their Communication with the *English*, they use Fire Arms. If they are engaged in War, which seldom is amongst themselves, but against the Neighbouring *Indians*, the Vanquished are sure to suffer from the insulting Victor, by burning or scalping the Skin and Hair from their Heads, in the Presence of the King, and their whole Nation, assembled for that Purpose.

They live in little Huts, called Wigwams, so low, that without stooping and creeping upon all Fours they cannot get into them.[7] As the *English* purchase Lands of them, they retire farther Westward from our Settlements.[8] Hunting is allowed to them and all others, there being no Lords of Manors to hamper them with their Privileges;[9] and here are

6. The spiritual beliefs of the Lenape were much more complex than Moraley portrays. See Kraft, *The Lenape*, 161–94.

7. The Lenape actually lived in a variety of structures, including wigwams and longhouses (ibid., 104–27, 214–15; Wacker, *Land and People*, 61).

8. By the time Moraley passed through the area, most of the Native Americans, demoralized by military defeat, the devastation of European diseases, and the continual growth and expansion of the white population, had sold or abandoned their lands and withdrawn westward, primarily to western Pennsylvania. See Kraft, *The Lenape*, 224–36; Wacker, *Land and People*, 84–88; and Daniel K. Richter, "A Framework for Pennsylvania Indian History," *Pennsylvania History* 57 (1990): 246–47.

9. The Pennsylvania custom of allowing hunting on unimproved private land was considered so important that it was written into the Pennsylvania Constitution of 1776 (Theodore Thayer, *Pennsylva-*

plenty of all Sorts of Venison, both cheap and good, and larger than ours.

Money is very scarce, being carried from Province to Province, from whence it never returns; so they are obliged to emit more new every three Years. *English* Money is the most valuable, one Guinea passing for Twenty-eight Shillings,[10] every Shilling for Eighteen-pence, Six-pence for Nine-pence, one Half-penny for a Penny; but as there are not enough to supply the Exigence of the State, both Paper and Parchment Money passes for current Coin, by the Authority of the Governor and Assembly; a Petition being lodged with the Governor, setting forth, That the Money is either defaced, or dispersed into the other Provinces; so that there is a Necessity of new Emissions, perhaps to the Value of 40 or 50,000 Pound.[11]

The Governor takes time to consider if their Allegation is true, and advises with his Council if it be convenient to grant them their Request; when after a mature Deliberation, he commonly gives his Consent, for which he receives a Premium, paid him first out of the new Coin, of about 2000 Pounds, and acquaints the Lords Commissioners of Trade and Plantations with the Affair, for their Approbation. Then Presses are set up, and the Money is coined, and deposited in the Loan Office, where Persons under Difficulties pawn their Lands, for such sums as they have Occasion for, and pay Interest. With this Interest the Proper Officers Sallaries are paid, and the Remainder serves to defray the Expenses of the State.

The Value of this Money is from one Shilling to five Pound, canton'd into Bills of one, two Shillings and Six-pence, three, five, six, ten, fifteen, twenty Shillings, three Pound, and five Pound Bills, of about four Inches long, and three Inches in breadth; and on divers Places are expressed the Value, with the Arms of every Province, and the Names of Persons who sign them, deputed by the Governor, to prevent Counterfeits.

The Governor of *Pennsilvania* has a salary of 2000 Pounds a Year

nia Politics and the Growth of Democracy, 1740–1776 [Harrisburg: Pennsylvania Historical and Museum Commission, 1953], 225).

10. A guinea was worth 21 shillings in England.

11. The assembly issued £30,000 Pennsylvania currency in 1729 and an additional £40,000 in 1731. In a pamphlet in 1729, Benjamin Franklin advocated a liberal paper-money policy (Leonard W. Labaree, ed., *The Papers of Benjamin Franklin*, 28 vols. [New Haven: Yale University Press, 1959–], 1:141).

allowed him, and receives five hundred Pounds a Year from the Independent Counties of *Newcastle, Kent*, and *Sussex*, where he presides in the Assembly, at certain Times in the Year.[12] This is the *Civil List*, and he has it granted from Year to Year, which is confirm'd to him every Session. He is nominated by the Heirs of the late *William Penn*, but confirmed by the King, and is seldom removed. His Perquisites arise from a Poll Tax, of Four Shillings in the Pound, from all single Persons that have been resident in the Province one Year; married Men pay only Two Shillings. He likewise receives Eight Shillings and Four-pence, for every Marriage License.

The Governor's Council consists of the most substantial Persons as to Figure and Fortune, and are to him the same as a House of Lords. The Commons are deputed from the Towns and Counties, and the Members, to qualify them to sit, must have either 1,000 Acres of Land, or fifteen hundred Pounds in Money. In their Proceedings, they endeavour to imitate the same Method as is used in the *British* Parliament; and here are Persons of Ingenuity and polite Literature. The Magistrates are not obliged to be of the Established Church, to qualify them to enjoy Posts of Honour and Profit. Here they discharge the Duties of their several Trusts, without regard to Difference of Religion or Party; both Quaker and Churchman living together in perfect Harmony.[13]

The Family of *Penn* have very great Respect paid them by all Sorts of Persons, tho' they have no share in the Administration of the Government Affairs. They received, when I was there, about 14,000 Pounds *per Annum*, for Quit Rent, as an acknowledgment to them as Propri-

12. Patrick Gordon served as deputy governor of Pennsylvania from 1726 to 1736. Moraley probably overstates the governor's salary, because Governor Evans (1703–9) estimated his annual income as only £300. William Penn acquired title to the three "lower" counties (now Delaware) in 1682 from the Duke of York. See Jean R. Soderlund, Richard S. Dunn, and Mary Maples Dunn, eds., *William Penn and the Founding of Pennsylvania 1680–1684: A Documentary History* (Philadelphia: University of Pennsylvania Press, 1983), 8; and Winfred Trexler Root, *The Relations of Pennsylvania with the British Government, 1696–1765* (1912; reprint, New York: AMS Press, 1969), 57.

13. Moraley exaggerates the suffrage and office-holding requirements in Pennsylvania and New Jersey. In colonial Pennsylvania, any male Christian who was at least twenty-one years old, two years resident in the province, and the owner of fifty acres (including twelve cleared) or £50 in property could vote and hold office. The governor's council was not the equivalent of the House of Lords, since it had no legislative functions and was confined to being an advisory body. See Thayer, *Pennsylvania Politics*, 4–6. In New Jersey, voting and office-holding requirements were less clearly stated and were sometimes subject to political maneuvering. However, the 1705 law stipulated that all freeholders could vote and that those who had £500 sterling in personal property were also eligible for membership in the House. See John E. Pomfret, *Colonial New Jersey: A History* (New York: Scribner's, 1973), 126.

etors, at about Five Shillings every hundred Acres. They have a fine Seat at *Pennsbury*, eight Miles from *Philadelphia*, near the River, but it is now in a ruinous Condition. It has a large Orchard, stored with Apples and Peach Trees. The Family built this House in One Thousand Six Hundred and Eighty Two. I was there in 1731.

This Province was settled upon them, on Account of a Debt due to Admiral *Penn*,[14] in consideration of Services done by him to the Government, till the Debt was discharged, and was granted by Charter from *Charles* the Second.[15] The present Proprietor is *Thomas Penn*, Esq., a worthy good-natur'd Gentlemen.[16]

The Laws here are the same as in *England*, as a Basis; but they have introduced so many By-ones, for the particular Government of Towns, as they pretend, for the more speedy Execution of Justice, that in some Cases destroys the Liberty of the Subject; nothing being more common than to see Men committed to Prison without legal Warrant, by the arbitrary Authority of the Magistrates.[17] I have been twice committed in this Manner, but one good Thing is to be observed, there being no vexatious Suits commenced upon frivolous Quarrels, which drains the Pockets of the lowest Class of Men in *England*: For upon the Appearance of a Quarrel, the Neighbours meet, in order to make an amicable Agreement, which being put to Arbitration, reconciles the Parties.

In the Towns as well as Country they are civil to all Strangers; and if they behave themselves well, will encourage them to stay among them, and marry. What induces many to stay, is the Cheapness of Provisions, and the Women, who are very handsome. Besides many have good Fortunes, perhaps Fifteen or Twenty Thousand Pounds.

The Quakers have a Custom of raising Money at their several Meet-

14. Admiral William Penn (1621–70) was the father of William Penn, founder of Pennsylvania.

15. Charles II granted the large tract of land to William Penn on March 4, 1681, partly in lieu of the £16,000 debt owed to Penn's father's estate (Soderlund et al., *William Penn*, 3; Joseph J. Kelly Jr., *Pennsylvania: The Colonial Years, 1681–1776* [Garden City, N.Y.: Doubleday, 1980], 17).

16. Thomas Penn (1702–75) was the son of William Penn.

17. The Pennsylvania criminal code concerning felonies was disallowed in 1718 and replaced by a law requiring the death penalty in accordance with English practice. Misdemeanors and the civil law were not affected by this change, so at times Pennsylvania and British practice diverged. See Alexander James Dallas, *Laws of the Commonwealth of Pennsylvania, from the Fourteenth Day of October, 1700*, 4 vols. (Philadelphia: Hall & Sellers, 1796), 1:133. John Murrin argues that American court procedures did not become Anglified until the late colonial period (John M. Murrin, "The Legal Transformation: The Bench and Bar of Eighteenth-Century Massachusetts," in Stanley N. Katz and John M. Murrin, eds., *Colonial America: Essays in Politics and Social Development*, 3rd ed. [New York: Knopf, 1983]). Of course, suspected runaway servants, slaves, and apprentices could be arrested by any sheriff. Although arrest warrants probably should have been issued, they were frequently neglected.

ings, as I observ'd before, with which they do many charitable Offices to the Poor and Indigent. I have experienc'd the Effects of their Benevolence. If any Person, though a Stranger, continues to do well, by preserving a good Character, and they have a good Opinion of them, they will enquire into his Circumstances, and if it appears he is distress'd in his Business for want of Stock, or necessary Implements to carry on his Trade, they will set him up out of this Money, without demanding any Security either by Bond or Promissory Note; and if he repays them, they will never give him any Trouble.

Their Marriages are very chargeable, many times the Wife's Fortune being expended at the Celebration of the Nuptials.[18] The Town Folks are generally invited to them, when all Kinds of Rarities are consum'd. Their Burials too are attended by all Sorts of People, both Whites and Blacks; and Hot Wine and Sugar Cakes[19] are dispers'd among them. I have partook of their Liberality on these Occasions. It is given to all Persons standing in the Streets, and sitting at their Doors. Their Ways of House-keeping are not much different from ours.

Cyder is the most plentiful here of all Liquors; besides which they have Mead, Methlegin, Perry, and Peach Drink.[20] The Beer [is] not good. *Madeira* Wine[21] is the only Wine us'd here. Rum is sold for Three-pence the Half-pint, or Ten-pence a Quart. Half a Pint of Rum being mix'd with three Half-pints of Water or Small Beer, makes *Bombo*; but mix'd with Cyder, makes *Sampson*, an intoxicating Liquor.

The Markets in all the Towns are well stor'd with all Sorts of Provisions, cheaper than at *Newcastle upon Tyne*. Fish is so plentiful, that large Pearch and Roach are sold for Three-pence a Dozen, and Trouts at the same Price. 'Tis dangerous fishing for them for the Water Snakes, one being forc'd to wade up to the Knees in the Runs where they are most plentiful. One day one *John Houghton*[22] of *Burlington* and myself, being distress'd for a *Sunday*'s Dinner, went a fishing and in twenty Minutes caught between us 140 Perch and Roach; and in returning home to his

18. Marriage ceremonies among Quakers in colonial America often were quite elaborate and costly. See J. William Frost, *The Quaker Family in Colonial America: A Portrait of the Society of Friends* (New York: St. Martin's Press, 1973), 174.

19. Sugar cakes are a sweetened or flavored bread.

20. All are alcoholic beverages. Mead and methlegin were made from a mixture of honey and water, and perry was fermented from the juice of pears.

21. A wine produced on the island of Madeira, located about four hundred miles from the northwest coast of Africa.

22. The Houghton family resided on the south side of High Street in Burlington; John Houghton lived in Hopewell Township, Burlington County, in 1741 (AIS).

Father's, to get 'em dress'd, we sold five Dozen of them for Fifteen-pence, and the Remainder serv'd six People for Dinner. The Money was laid out in Rum and Sugar, to wash them down. These sort of Fish are generally 10 or 12 Inches long.

The Country is generally level, but woody, having but few mountaneous Parts, (they lying more Westward, where are no Inhabitants) and produces many sorts of Trees, as Hiccory, Oak, which together make the best and most durable Firing; Sassafras, White and Red Cedar, Ash, Pines, Limes; abundance of Grapes, both of the Red and Muscadel Kind; plenty of wild Peaches, but sour. The Garden Peach grows upon standing Trees as large as Apple Trees. I have seen eleven Sorts, but the Early Peach is best. The next in Goodness is the Plumb Peach. Mulberries are of two Sorts, Black and White, but not near so good as the *English* ones, and are much smaller. Morello and Black Cherries[23] are very good and cheap, so are all the other Sorts.

Here are Currants and Rasberries, Strawberries, Blackberries, with Artichokes and Asparagus, Collyflowers, Turnips, Parsnips, Beans and Peas, as good as any in *England*; Potatoes, *Jerusalem* Artichokes, Pomegranates, Muskmellons, and Yams, better than Potatoes; also *Indian* Corn, which boil'd young, and eaten with Butter, is as good as Chestnuts, having almost the very same Taste.

In the Summer time, which begins to appear about the First of *May*, the long Winter on a sudden disappears, and the mellifluous Flowers and Plants, with their fragrant Smell, gratify the Senses with a wonderful Diversity, and the melodious Songsters of the Woods, the Fields and Groves, chant forth their Joy in warbling Notes, forming even a terrestrial Paradise. Then a clear Sky, and constant refreshing Breezes, revive the glad Planter, and he no more remembers the cold Winter's pinching Frost, but chearfully cultivates his teeming Soil, expecting from his Labour a grateful Return for his Industry.

This Country, were it not for the Uncertainty of the windy Weather, which often disappoints the industrious Planter, would be one of the noblest in the Universe; but the North East Wind that generally blows for near three Quarters of the Year, is the Occasion of it. One hot Day is succeeded by a cold one, which checks and pinches the Fruits of the Earth, and often retards their Growth.

During the Summer, which lasts but three Months, the Sun burns

23. Morello is a cherry with a bitter taste, and black cherries usually are wild cherries.

and parches the Earth, which opening, receives the descending Rain, and fertilizes it. The Soil in many Places is like Garden Ground, being from three to five Foot deep of Black Mould, which Fatness produces great Quantities of all Sorts of Corn and Grain.[24] In the Year 1730, eight Persons dropp'd down dead in one Day, at *Philadelphia*, by reason of the excessive Heat of the Weather.[25] It is dangerous to drink Water at this Season, hot Liquor being more proper, to allay the Thirst.

Then Thunder and Lightning, with terrible Gusts of Wind and Rain, descend, and surprise the Inhabitants. The first Beginning is, a violent Storm of Wind arises, obliging the People to secure their Windows, to prevent their being shatter'd. It then blows so hard, as often lifts the People off the Ground. Then succeeds a violent Rain, which continues but for about ten Minutes; then Thunder and Lightning, which clarifies the Air. After which appears a Serenity in the Sky seldom seen in *England*. Then the green Fields and verdant Meadows display their several Beauties, advantageous to the joyful Shepherd.

Every where are to be found pleasant useful Rivulets of salubrious Water, and the larger streams over-flow the adjacent Meadows, rendering them prolifick.—Thus has the benign Creator display'd his Power and Goodness in the Production of all his Works.

The Winters are so severly cold as benumbs the Inhabitants, and begins so early, that from the Fourth of *November* to the Twenty-fifth of *March*, in 1730, the great River *Delaware* was hard frozen, Coaches and Carts passing it on either Side.[26] One *Andrew Galloway*[27] an *Irishman*, and myself, going over in a Sled, the Ice broke, and he was drown'd.

The Cold was so excessive, that the People were obliged to keep [in]

24. New Jersey actually contained extremely variable soils, although the area surrounding Burlington was among the best in the colony (Wacker, *Land and People*, 10–12).

25. The month of July 1734 was the hottest in this period; five people were reported to have died of the heat (John F. Watson, *Annals of Philadelphia, and Pennsylvania, in the Olden Time*, 3 vols. [Philadelphia: Stuart, 1899], 2:353).

26. Europeans frequently remarked on the cold weather in the Mid-Atlantic region and noted that the Delaware River often iced during the winter months (e.g., Kalm, *America of 1750*, 2:677–78). The winter of 1733–34 was one of the coldest in the eighteenth century. The Delaware River did not begin to thaw until mid-February, and it was not navigable until the second week in March. See David M. Ludlum, *Early American Winters, 1604–1820* (Boston: American Meteorological Society, 1966), 47–48; Samuel Hazard, "Effects of Climate on the Navigation of the River Delaware, 1681–1828," *Hazard's Register of Pennsylvania* 2 (1828): 23; and reports from the *New England Weekly Journal* (Boston), March 19, 1734.

27. Andrew Galloway appeared among the many debtors listed in the inventory of Enoch Fenton, butcher, of Burlington in 1732 (Wills, 2:173).

their Houses; and all Business was at a stand. Divers Persons lost the Use of their Limbs for some Days, during the Sharpness of the Frost, it being more than ordinary Cold. I was forced to carry Wood for Firing, was pinched to such a Degree, that I thought myself unhappy in living. I often reflected on the Prodigal Son, and wished with him to eat the Husks that were given the Swine in his Father's House.[28]

During my stay in these Parts of the World, I have experienced the Mutability and Inconstancy of human Affairs; for from a tollerable State of Life, I have been reduced to Poverty, then have been up-set, then down: In short, I have been the Tennis-ball of Fortune,[29] and may say, with *Hudibrass*,[30]

> *I that was once as great as* Caesar,
> *Am now reduced to* Nebuchadnezzar:
> *Like as a Dog that turns a Spit,*
> *Bestirs himself, and plies his Feet,*
> *To climb the Wheel; but all in vain,*
> *His own Weight brings him down again.*
> *But still he's in the self same Place,*
> *Where at his setting out he was.*

But I being of a Temper not easily cast down by Adversity, continue, though down, and wait for a Trump Card to repay me what I had lost.

28. The story of the prodigal son is from Luke 15:11–32.

29. John Webster expressed similar popular sentiments in "The Duchess of Malfi" in 1614: "We are merely the stars' tennis-balls, struck and bandied / Which way please them" (Esther Cloudman Dunn, ed., *Eight Famous Elizabethan Plays* [New York: Modern Library, 1950], 537).

30. *Hudibras* is Samuel Butler's seventeenth-century verse-satire on Puritanism. Moraley accurately quotes the initial two lines of the canto entitled "An Heroical Epistle of Hudibras to His Lady." The balance of Moraley's poem, with its shift from a regal to a homely metaphor, is not from *Hudibras* and may well be an original conceit by Moraley. The awkward rhyme scheme (spit/feet, vain/again, place/was) would tend to rule out a more proficient poet as the author. See Samuel Butler, *Hudibras, in Three Parts, Written in the Time of the Late Wars [1678]* (Baltimore: Lucas & Nicklin, 1812), 304.

8 END OF SERVITUDE IN PENNSYLVANIA—"A ROVING TARTER"—COURTING ADVENTURE—TRENT TOWN AND BURLINGTON—ENCOUNTER WITH A PANTHER—DETAINED FOR A RUNAWAY—JOURNEY TO NEW YORK—AN INDIAN KING—THE GOVERNOR OF NEW YORK—PURSUED BY CREDITORS.

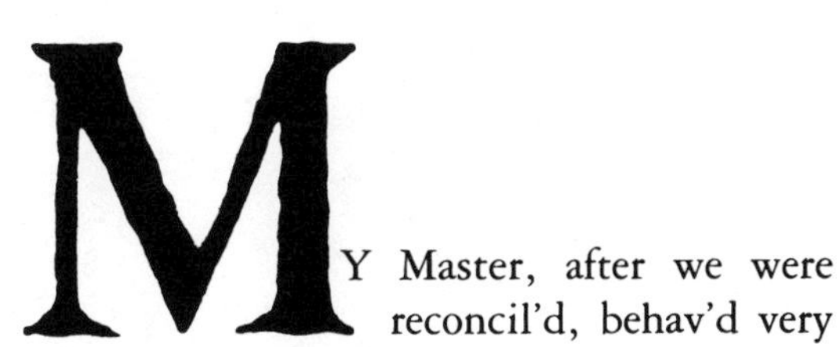

MY Master, after we were reconcil'd, behav'd very civilly to me, and I liv'd very happy, to the Expiration of my Servitude. He had a Share in an Iron Work at a Place call'd *Mount Holly*,[1] about seven Miles from *Burlington*, where I was sent to Work. Here I have had many a merry Day. Sometimes I have acted the Blacksmith; at other times, I have work'd in the Water, stark naked, among Water Snakes. Sometimes I was a Cow Hunter in the Woods, and sometimes I got Drunk for Joy that my Work was ended.

At last this Iron Work was perfected and the Time of my Servitude expir'd, and I became free. 'Tis impossible to express the Satisfaction I found at being releas'd from the precarious Humour and Dependence of

1. Isaac Pearson, Mahlon Stacy, and John Burr purchased 345 acres of land in 1730 and built a furnace and forge at Mount Holly on the south branch of Rancocas Creek (Boyer, *Early Forges and Furnaces*, 128ff.). It was a relatively isolated place, and only 281 people lived in the rural township including Mount Holly in 1709 (John Rodgers, "Census of Northampton, Burlington County, 1709," *Proceedings of the New Jersey Historical Society* 4 [1849]: 33–36).

my Master. He accouter'd me in an indifferent Manner, and gave me my Discharge, to find out a new Way of Living.[2] I then went to *Philadelphia* and served one *Edmund Lewis*, a brisk young Clock-maker; but he being unsettled, and of a roving Temper (*like Master, like Man*!), I left him, and liv'd with Mr *Graham*, a Watch-maker, newly arriv'd, and Nephew to the famous Mr *Graham* in *Fleet-street*.[3] With him I continued ten Weeks, at Ten Shillings *per* Week Wages, and my Board found me;[4] but he designing to settle at *Antegoa*,[5] I left him.

Then I roam'd about like a Roving *Tartar*,[6] for the Convenience of Grazing, and for three Weeks had no Abiding Place. In the Nights I was forc'd to skulk about the Extremity of the Town, where I lay in a Hay-loft. In the Day time, I got Victuals of several of my Companions from *London*. Then, by their Help, I courted an old ugly Maid, who had got good store of Pewter and Brass.[7] The Match was agreed, and a Day appointed to put me in possession of her Moveables:[8] But the very Night before the Marriage was to be celebrated, she gave me a Gold Ring to take the Bruises out,[9] and accidentally meeting with some of my Acquaintance, they got the Ring from me, sold it, and spent the Money; so I lost my Sweet-heart.

But this Life not being likely to last long, and the People's Good-nature beginning to cool, I set my Wits to Work how to get home. But

2. That is, Moraley received inexpensive clothing as part of the "freedom dues" when his period of servitude expired.

3. William Graham, nephew of George Graham, was present in Philadelphia circa 1733; see John Edwards, *The Complete Checklist of American Clock and Watchmakers, 1640–1950* (Stratford, Conn.: New England Publishing, 1977), 19. A Fellow of the Royal Society and author of many scientific papers, George Graham (1673–1751) was a famous watchmaker and inventor. His shop stood at the Dial and One Crown in Fleet Street, London. See G. H. Baillie, C. Clutton, and C. A. Ilbert, *Britten's Old Clocks and Watches and Their Makers* (New York: Dutton, 1956), 278–80.

4. Food was provided as part of the wages.

5. Antigua, an island in the West Indies.

6. A strolling vagabond.

7. The woman may have been Elizabeth Paris, a recent widow and a brass founder. She advertised for a runaway apprentice in the June 11, 1730, issue of the *Pennsylvania Gazette* and died in the summer of 1741 (*Pennsylvania Gazette*, August 27, 1741).

8. That is, to wed, for once Moraley was married he legally would have owned his wife's property.

9. Gold rings blessed by a priest on Good Friday, and sometimes inscribed with Bible verses, were given as gifts and used for betrothals. These "cramp-rings" were believed to have the power to cure various maladies. See John R. Gillis, *For Better, for Worse: British Marriages, 1600 to the Present* (New York: Oxford University Press, 1985), 62; and W. Carew Hazlitt, *Faiths and Folklore of the British Isles: A Descriptive and Historical Dictionary*, 2 vols. (1903; reprint, New York: Benjamin Blom, 1965), 1:154.

not presently hearing of a Ship bound for *England*, I was reduc'd to such Extremity, that I look'd like the Picture of bad Luck, and so thin, that you might have seen my Ribs through my Skin, and I was greatly afraid of a Consumption.[10] However, having some Acquaintance in the Country, I went about cleaning Clocks and Watches, and follow'd the Occupation of a Tinker;[11] but not being well vers'd in that Trade, where I mended one Hole, I was sure to make another.

But this Life serving only for the present, did not afford me a constant Supply; so in the Intervals was forc'd to spend, when I came back, what I had earn'd in these sort of Roamings. It never cost me any Money, by way of Expense; I was welcome every where, though unknown, and always recommended to Business from Place to Place, where I had Variety of Entertainment, always endeavouring to ingratiate myself into the People's Favour by a modest and decent Behaviour, which, with relating Stories when desir'd, and my giving them an Account of *England*, gain'd me the Reputation of an intelligent Man, though upon Occasion I could rake with the best of them, and change my Note as proper Time offer'd.

I remember I was going to a Place call'd *Cross-field*, between *Trent Town* and *Burlington*,[12] to mend a Clock, being bare-foot and bare-legg'd; and after I had acquitted myself in the best Manner, and receiv'd Ten Shillings for my Pains, I went to *Trent Town*, a pretty neat Place, containing about 200 Houses, and lay there two Nights, after I had clean'd two Clocks. This Town stands twenty Miles from *Burlington*, near the River *Delaware*, having many handsome Houses, and rich Inhabitants.

Here I found out the young Lady whom I sav'd from drowning, who, by the Death of her Father, was left possess'd of a Fortune of Three Thousand Pounds.[13] She ask'd me to take a Dinner with her, which I did, and after that drank Tea with her, when she gave me Three Pound, and desir'd to know how Things stood with me; which having satisfied her in, I took my Leave of her, in order to return home.

10. A "consumption" described a number of different diseases that wasted the body. Often the disease was pulmonary tuberculosis.

11. An artisan who mends pots, kettles, and other household utensils made from tin, a base metal not used by watchmakers.

12. Moraley probably means the town of Crosswicks, between Burlington and Trenton (see Map 2).

13. Hannah Lambert was the daughter of Thomas Lambert. When he died in 1733, she shared his estate valued at nearly £5,000 (not including real estate) with her three sisters (Wills, 2:42–43).

About four Miles from *Trent Town*, passing along a spacious Road, I espy'd a Beast at a Distance, and observ'd his Eyes were fix'd upon me. I was so terribly affrighted, that, to prevent any Danger, I climb'd up a large Oak Tree and secur'd myself in the Branches. When the Beast drew near, I perceiv'd that it was a Panther, about the Largeness of a Mastiff Dog. He set his Fore Feet against the Tree, and attempted to climb up. I was so terrified at this, that I shiver'd, and all my Passions were at Work: But after he had tried to ascend in vain, by falling down twice, he roar'd, and gently left the Place.

It was near two Hours before I ventur'd to descend, for fear he should have conceal'd himself, in order to surprise me; and when I did venture down, I walk'd so warily, that it was near two Hours more before I reach'd the next House, which was but two Miles from the Place. This prov'd to be the Habitation of Mr *Isaac Horner*,[14] a *Yorkshire* Gentleman of Substance. I told him of this Adventure, at which he laugh'd, and said he had been in the same Circumstances. After Mr *Horner* had treated me with the best his House afforded, I went to Bed. In the morning I set out for home, but miss'd my Way.

Here are so many Cross Roads, which makes it exceeding difficult to keep the Right one; for instead of taking the Right, I struck into a broad Road, which, I was afterwards told, leads to a Wood of Pines, that grow close together, over-shadows the Road, and prevents any Communication with the Sky. In these Woods, Bears, Wolves, and Panthers range about, often putting the Traveller into a Fear. If I had continued this Way, I should not have met with a House till I came to *Salem*, a Town near the *Capes*, which was near two hundred Miles from me.[15]

After I had journied about eight Miles in the Road, not finding any Appearance of any House or Farm to enquire of, and fearing the Consequence of being lost in the Woods, I returned, happily for me, and guessed at a Road, which led me to *Allons Town*, a pitiful dirty Hole; where I arrived after nine Hours Travel, not meeting with any one to direct me. I drank some Cyder, eat some Hung Beef, and got Directions to *Recklish Town*, seated on the River, eight Miles from *Trent Town*,

14. Isaac Horner lived in Burlington County between 1704 and 1739 (AIS).

15. Moraley was indeed lost, because Salem is not on the land route to the Capes, although the town would be passed when one was sailing down the Delaware River. The Capes are about 100 miles from Trenton; Allentown, New Jersey, lies southeast of Trenton (see Map 2). Recklesstown is now Chesterfield, New Jersey.

where I was known. Here I came and was received well. It is a pretty large neat Place, of about Fifty Houses.

From thence I took the Right Road, and lost it, which so perplexed me, and being dispirited I broke out into the following Expressions, *If ever I have the good Fortune to reach my Native Country, I am resolved to reform my Life and Conversation, in such a Manner, as not to suffer a sinful Thought to harbour in my Breast.* Night coming on, I was in a sad Taking, reflected on my former Condition of Life, and, comparing it with the present, said, *I that was brought up so tenderly by my indulgent Parents, am now reduced to the most deplorable Circumstances.*

Thus ruminating with myself, at last I discovered a Light at a great Distance, and endeavour'd to make up to it. After some Difficulty I got to it, and it proved to be the Habitation of *John Montgomery*, a *Scotchman*, where I was taken up for a Runaway, and detain'd all Night.[16] However I got a good Supper, consisting of hot Wheaten Bread and Milk, and a hot Apple Pye. In the Morning I was carried on a Horse by two Men to *Burlington*, where my former master cleared me, by producing my Indentures; and the Men returned home, but with this difference, that they had their Labour for their Pains, and Money out of Pocket upon my Account.

Three Days after this Adventure, I worked Journey Work with *Peter Bishop*,[17] a Blacksmith, for eight Shillings a Week, and Necessaries found me, as Lodging, Meat and Drink. I worked at the great Hammer, in making Horse Shoes, Horseshoe Nails, rounding of Ship Bolts, sharpening Coulters[18] for the Plow, &c. This Life I followed six Week, and out of my Earnings bought a fine shirt, the first I wore since my Departure from *England*. Many a hard Day I have had at this Employment, but necessity enabled me to surmount all Difficulties.

During this employ, my Creditors at *Philadelphia*, where I owed trifling Debts, such as Three or Four Shillings to each, but amounted in the Whole to above Eight Pound, found me out, and threaten'd me with summoning me before the Magistrate. This obliged me to leave my Blacksmith, for at that Time I could never hear a Dun with Pa-

16. John Montgomerie (d. 1733), a resident of Burlington County, had recently served as governor of New York and New Jersey (Wills, 2:342).

17. Peter Bishop, blacksmith, appears in many Burlington records. Thomas Wetherill, apparently Bishop's father-in-law, resided in Burlington City at his death in 1759 and owned property in several counties in New Jersey (Wills, 3:354).

18. A plow's iron blade, which cuts through the soil.

tience; so I steer'd my Course for *New York*, to avoid their Impertinence. After three Days march, I arrived at *Elizabeth Town*, about eighteen Miles from *New York*. Near which Place, as I was walking in the Road, I espy'd a new Brick House, and a Negro working in an adjoining Field, who called to me, and asked me if I would not come and see his Master, who was an *Indian* King.

Little Persuasion serv'd, being weary; so I went with him, and was admitted to the Royal Presence. The King was sitting by the Fire Side, upon a Carpet, attended by two bought Servants, and Three Negro Slaves, drinking Rum. His name was *Yo-Taen-San-Lo*, King of the *Chiapase*. After paying him a Respect due to his Quality, he desired me to sit down and smoak a Pipe, and order'd Pipes and Tobacco to be brought; and Rum, a Glass of which being handed to me, I soon dispatched it. He kindly ask'd me if I was an *Englishman*. I told him, I was, and born at *London*. Then he drank to me again, and I pledg'd him a second Time. He invited me to Dinner, and a Quarter of Lamb was roasted.

After Dinner Punch was set upon the Carpet, when we drank heartily. Then he desired me to relate to him the Manners and Customs of the *English*, with the State of our King; which I did, wonderfully magnifying every Thing, and making our King ten Times greater than he is. After drinking three or four Glasses more, I would have taken my Leave of him, but he desired me to stay an Hour longer, which I did; and then took notice of his Furniture, which was good Chairs and Stools, provided for Strangers, for they never use any themselves, nor Beds.

At last I got leave to depart, and made the best of my Way to *New York*, where I arrived that Night. In the Morning I waited upon the Governor, and presented to him my Credentials from my first Master, as to my Business. He order'd me to continue at his House till further Notice, and the Servants helped me to what I stood in need of.

Colonel *Crosby* the Governor,[19] was an *Irishman*, and formerly a common Soldier; but being a graceful Man, had the Address to gain the Affection of Lord *Halifax's* Sister, and married her, which raised him to the Posts he enjoys. He had two Daughters, both handsome Ladies. The Eldest was married to the Lord *Augustus Fitzroy*, Second Son to the Duke of *Grafton*. The youngest is unmarried. This Marriage was just then

19. William Cosby (ca. 1695–1736) served as governor of New York from 1731 to 1736.

discovered, which gave a great deal of Uneasiness to the Family, because the Father was a Stranger to it; but the Matter was soon made up by the Lord *Baltimore* with the Duke of *Grafton*.

The next Day the Governor order'd me two Clocks to clean, for which he gave me two Pistoles,[20] and recommended me to several Gentlemen of Figure, from whom I got Money. But my Creditors joining together, made one Debt of it, and followed me to *New York*, by a Letter to an Attorney; which I having Notice of, immediately apply'd to Capt. *Ingoldsby*, Commander of the Fort, and Son to the Late Lieutenant General *Ingoldsby*, Commander of her late Majesty Queen *Anne's* Troops in *Ireland*, who admitted me as a Soldier: So that the Attorney applying to the Captain, had no Remedy.

Escaping this Snare, I continued at *New York*, and liv'd as a Servant with a *Spanish* Gentleman, named *Don Roderigo de Almeria*, of *Valentia*. I liv'd a very sober, retir'd Life, and obtain'd this Gentleman's Favour, by my Assiduity in serving him. He made me his Confident, and related to me his Adventures, which are, in his own Words, as follows.

20. A Spanish gold coin that varied in value, a pistole was worth approximately 15 English shillings during most of the early eighteenth century.

9 THE VALENTIAN; OR, FAITHFUL LOVER

AT *Valentia*, chief City of the Kingdom of that Name, the richest, pleasant, and most fertile Kingdom in *Spain*, liv'd *Don Roderigo de Almeria*, descended from the Dukes of *Medina Coeli*, First Peers of *Spain*. He enjoy'd a plentiful Estate, besides an honourable Post he held under the King, being Comptroller of the Finances of *Valentia*. He married *Donna Jacinta*, Daughter of *Don Pedro Torruga*, a Gentleman of Fortune at *Malaga*. By her he had three Sons, myself being the youngest, and named after him. My eldest Brother, *Don Sancho*, was sent into the Wars against the Emperor.

I continued at home with my Father, being design'd for a religious Habit; but that Life not suiting with my Inclination, I expostulated with my Father, and told him, I was inclin'd to follow the Law, notwithstanding an Education was given me to qualify me for the former Profession. My Father giving Ear to my Request, sent me to *Malaga*, where I studied the Law under the Direction of *Don Manuel Lopes de Gusman*, and acquir'd, by my Assiduity, a general Applause.

There lived in the Neighbourhood, a Lady, Daughter of a considerable Banker, nam'd, *Sebestian de la Vega*. She was young and beautiful, and possess'd of all the good Qualities which seldom fail of making a complete Woman. I conceiv'd a Passion for her, infinitely beyond Expression. My first Sight of her was at a *Villa*, some small Distance from *Malaga*; and at my Return, I made it my chief Business to find out the Mistress of my Affections, which I soon effected by means of an old *Duena* who was kept in the Family.

At this Time I made a Figure suitable to the Grandeur of my Family, having large Remittances from my Father. This *Duena* passing by near the House where I liv'd, I gave her a Letter, with some Money, promising, if she acquitted herself faithfully, I'd make her a handsome Recompence. She promis'd me she would, and parted. I follow'd her to the House, and perceiv'd she deliver'd my Letter to the Object of my Wishes. I waited some Days, expecting her Answer; when a Servant brought me a Billet, and left me abruptly. I hastily open'd it, and read the following Words.

To Don Roderigo de Almeria.

SIR,

I Am very much surpris'd to find a Gentleman should express a Passion for a Lady with whom he has not the least Acquaintance. For me, I am under the Direction of a Father, to whom I owe all possible Love and Obedience; and can never grant a Heart to any other, without his Approbation. You are at your own Disposal, and unless you apply in a proper Manner, can receive no Admittance from

JAQUELINA.

This answer'd my Expectation, and I was as much charm'd with her Prudence as her Person; but not knowing which Way to apply to her Father, ten thousand Thoughts revolv'd in my Mind. But he having, soon after, a Contest at Law, my good Fortune brought me acquainted with him; for by the Recommendation of a neighbouring Gentleman, I became his Advocate, had an Opportunity of visiting him, and by him was introduc'd to the Acquaintance of the incomparable *Donna Jaquelina*. The Law-suit was ended to his Advantage, and I received the Applause of the Court, and the Thanks of the Family.

This made *Don Sebestian* enquire after my Family, and being informed to his Satisfaction, told *Donna Jaquelina*, she must not look upon me as a Person necessitated to follow the Law, but as one descended of the first House in *Spain*; which coming to my hearing, by the Means of the old *Duena*, I received at all Times, an easy Admittance, which imbolden'd me to declare my Passion to her the first favourable Opportunity that should offer.

The next Day as I was passing by the Church, called *Notre Dame de Dios*, I perceived a Lady advancing towards me, and discovered her to be the charming *Jaquelina*; and putting a Face upon it, I addressed her in the most civil Manner. Madam, says I, you are sensible of the entire Affection I have for you, and hope you will give me leave to return you my Thanks for the many Happinesses I enjoy in your Conversation. I was going on when she stopped me, by turning short, and stepping into the Church.

This affected me to such a Degree, that I became Thunderstruck, but composing myself, I stay'd till she return'd; and then accosting her with the greatest Respect, begged her Pardon for my Rudeness, and declared to her, in the sincerest Manner, that from the first Time I ever saw her, I became her Slave, and that no Consideration could prevail with me to withdraw my Affection.

A Declaration of this Nature surprized the lovely *Jaquelina*, but recovering herself. from her Confusion, and, blushing, said, Sir, I am subject to the Obedience of a tender Father, and without his Consent can never part with a Heart intirely at his Disposal. I then told her I was the Person to whom she directed a Billet, and protested that I wou'd sacrifice to her all other Considerations. We parted, and I returned home.

A few Days after *Don Sebestian* invited me to his House, when I received a Proof of his good Intentions. He declared to me, that as he had an only Daughter, he had some Inclination to dispose of her, and if I would accept of the Proposal, he should think himself honoured by such an Alliance. I humbly thanked him for his Offer, and told him, I intended to have asked the Favour of him, but was glad to find he had such a good Opinion of me, and accepted his Offer. After which I told her what had passed, and she with some reluctancy yielded to my Wishes, and a Day was appointed for the Solemnization of the Nuptials.

Before this an unlucky Accident happen'd, that made me the most miserable of Mankind. The Arrival of my second Brother, *Don Frederick*, who, with a magnificent Equipage, attracted the Eyes of the Citizens of *Malaga*. He took up his Residence at the Palace of the *Count de Mon-*

temar, the Governor, where I repaired to congratulate him on his safe Arrival. He received me with an Affection suitable to the Relation between us; when I told him of my intended Marriage, and invited him to grace my Nuptials with his Presence.

Some Days after I took him along with me, and introduced him into the House of *Don Sebestian*; where, on my Account, he met with a noble Reception. But after some few Days, I perceived I was received at the House with Coldness, and soon after was denyed Admittance, being told my Brother was more welcome. I upbraided him with his Breach of Friendship; but he denyed he had any Design to supplant me.

Soon after he married *Jaquelina*, which when I heard, I resolved to leave *Malaga*. To which Intent, I sold off all my Moveables, and, unknown either to my Brother or Acquaintance, left the Place, and went to my Father at *Valentia*, whom I made acquainted with my Brother's deceitful Dealings. He pacified me in the most moving Terms, and said, He would advance my Fortune, advising me to go to *Naples*.

Shortly after I sail'd with a Cargo of about Eight Thousand Pieces of Eight; but was taken by an *Algerine* Pirate, and carried to *Algiers*, where I continued a Slave three Years, and underwent inexpressible Hardships. But my Father hearing of my Disaster, soon redeemed me for 500 Pistoles, and I returned to *Valentia*.

I went afterwards with a Cargo to *Florida*; but that Place being unhealthy, I went to the *English* Colonies, and settled at *New York*, where I heard of the Death of my Second Brother. I then resolved to leave *America*, and sail'd in a *Dutch* Vessel bound to *Spain*. After a tedious Voyage, we arrived at *Gibraltar* where my Father gave me a welcome Reception, and desired me not to think of parting from him. Soon after News was brought us of the Death of my Elder Brother; so I became universal Heir to my Father's Estate.

The former Disappointment I met with as to *Jaquelina*, had not cured me, for now I was resolved to renew my Suit; to which Intent I stole from my Father, under Pretence of a Visit to *Don Hieronimo Gonzalez*, President of *Malaga*; and being attended by a Valet, set forward, and arrived there, where I inquired after her.

One Day as I was walking near the Arsenal, I perceived her in a Widow's Dress, and making an Obeisance, cryed, Dear *Jaquelina!* It is impossible to conceive the Confusion she was in at the Sight of me. She fixed her Eyes on me, and said, *Don Roderigo!* I recovered myself from my first surprize, and desired her to relate to me her Father's Unkindness. She protested to me, that from the first Time I addressed her, she conceived an Esteem for me, and what she did, was by compulsion of her Father; and since my Departure, she was under the greatest Concern for my Welfare.

Then she desired me to stay with her, telling me, That since the Death of my Brother, she had resolved to give her Heart to no other Person but my self; and that all she had was at my Disposal. I caused Articles of Marriage to be drawn, but an Objection was made as to the Validity of my Marriage; when I applied to the Archbishop of *Toledo* for a Dispensation, who procured me a Bull from *Rome*, invalidating my Brother's Marriage, upon the Account of a Pre-contract between myself and *Donna Jaquelina*.

I lived many Years with her, but Death parted us, which so sensible afflicted me, that I resolved to leave the World, and retire to a Monastry. Before this my Father died, when I sold my Estate, and gave the greatest Part to the Poor. Here I resigned myself to the Will of God, renouncing the Vanities of this troublesome World; but happening to find a Book wrote by the Archbishop of *Canterbury*, Dr. *Tillotson*, which levelled at the *Romish* Superstition, I became a Convert, and resolved to escape.[1] So with some Difficulty I transported myself to *London*, where I publickly renounced the Errors of the Church of *Rome*.

From *London* I embarked for *New York*, where I advanced my Fortune by Trade; but having an Inclination to spend the Remainder of my Day at *London*, in order to be thoroughly initiated into the Principles of the *Reformed Religion*, I now wait for a Ship to transport me thither for that Intent.

1. Dr. John Tillotson (1630–94) was Archbishop of Canterbury and author of a polemic against Roman Catholicism, "The Rule of Faith" (1666).

10 DEPARTURE FROM NEW YORK—DUCKING WITCHES AT MOUNT HOLLY—LOADING SHIP—JOURNEY TO MARYLAND—ENCOUNTER WITH A HORN SNAKE—ASSISTS A MOTHER AND TWO CHILDREN—DANGER FROM CREDITORS—SETS SAIL FOR IRELAND—THE MAN WITH THREE WIVES.

FTER I had continued with this Gentleman some time, I returned towards *Burlington*, and went and lived with my first Master, who sent me to *Mount Holly*, where I was witness to one of the strangest Pieces of Folly that was ever acted. Certain old Women, of Melancholick Physognomy,[1] had got the Character of Witches; and being questioned on that Account, and not able to clear themselves, were obliged to undergo a Ducking, in order to prove whether or no they were such.

The Notion run, if they sunk, they were no Witches; but if they swam, they were, and shou'd be punished as such. But they miraculously escaped the Censure of the Law, by sinking, tho' they remained a considerable Time on the Surface of the Water. But this not satisfying one *Jonathan Wright*,[2] he proposed to weigh them in Scales against the

1. A kind of madness evidenced in facial features.

2. On Jonathan Wright, see Appendix H.

Bible, and concluded, if they were Witches, they would not weigh so heavy as the Bible; but to the Surprise of the Beholders, they weighed down both Prophets and Apostles.[3]

After this foolish Adventure, I went back to *Burlington*, and lived again with the Blacksmith. This being the Time they gather the *Indian* Corn into their Grannaries, the Townspeople were busy in husking it for that Purpose. The Neighbours assist one another in stripping the Corn from the Husks, and are treated with Rum and Punch; but Persons of Figure provide a grand Entertainment. Every Night, for a Fortnight, I was busy at one or other of these Meetings.

I now began to be heartily tir'd with these Ramblings, and endeavoured to make Friends with Masters of Ships, in order to get my Passage. One Morning, as I was forging a Horse Shoe, a grave Quaker, one *Thomas Wetheril*, of *Workington*, in *Cumberland*, told me, He found the Business I follow'd would do little for me, and advis'd me to return Home, where he heard I had considerable Relations. He said he had recommended me to Capt. *Peel*, whose Ship then lay at the Key, and would sail in about five Weeks.

I who had before resolv'd to embrace the first Opportunity that offer'd readily entered into his Measures, immediately left the Horse Shoe unfinished, and went to the Ship, where the Captain was, and told him Mr *Wetheril* had sent me. He ask'd me if I was a Sailor; if not, if I would undertake to be Cook on board, he would give me my Passage, and on our arrival at *Ireland*, assist me with Money, to enable me to go to *Newcastle*. I immediately struck a Bargain, and at his Desire assisted the Crew in stowing the Ship with Logs, Hogsheads, and Pipe Staves,[4] he giving me Liberty to leave the Ship when any Business in my Way offer'd.

But the most difficult Task I had to undertake was splitting of Wood for Firing. This Wood was four Feet in Length; and the Materials for splitting, were an Ax and a Wedge. I was so awkward in my first Essay, that I feared I should not be able to compleat my Task, and consequently lose my Passage; which the Master perceiving, laugh'd, and generously gave me such Directions as enabled me to acquit Myself manfully, which I did in three Days, to his and my own Satisfaction.

3. A story about this event also appeared in the *Pennsylvania Gazette*, October 15–22, 1730. A more complete discussion of the episode and the reprinted newspaper article are available in Appendix H.

4. Hogsheads were large casks, and pipe staves were boards used for making pipes to hold liquids, primarily wine.

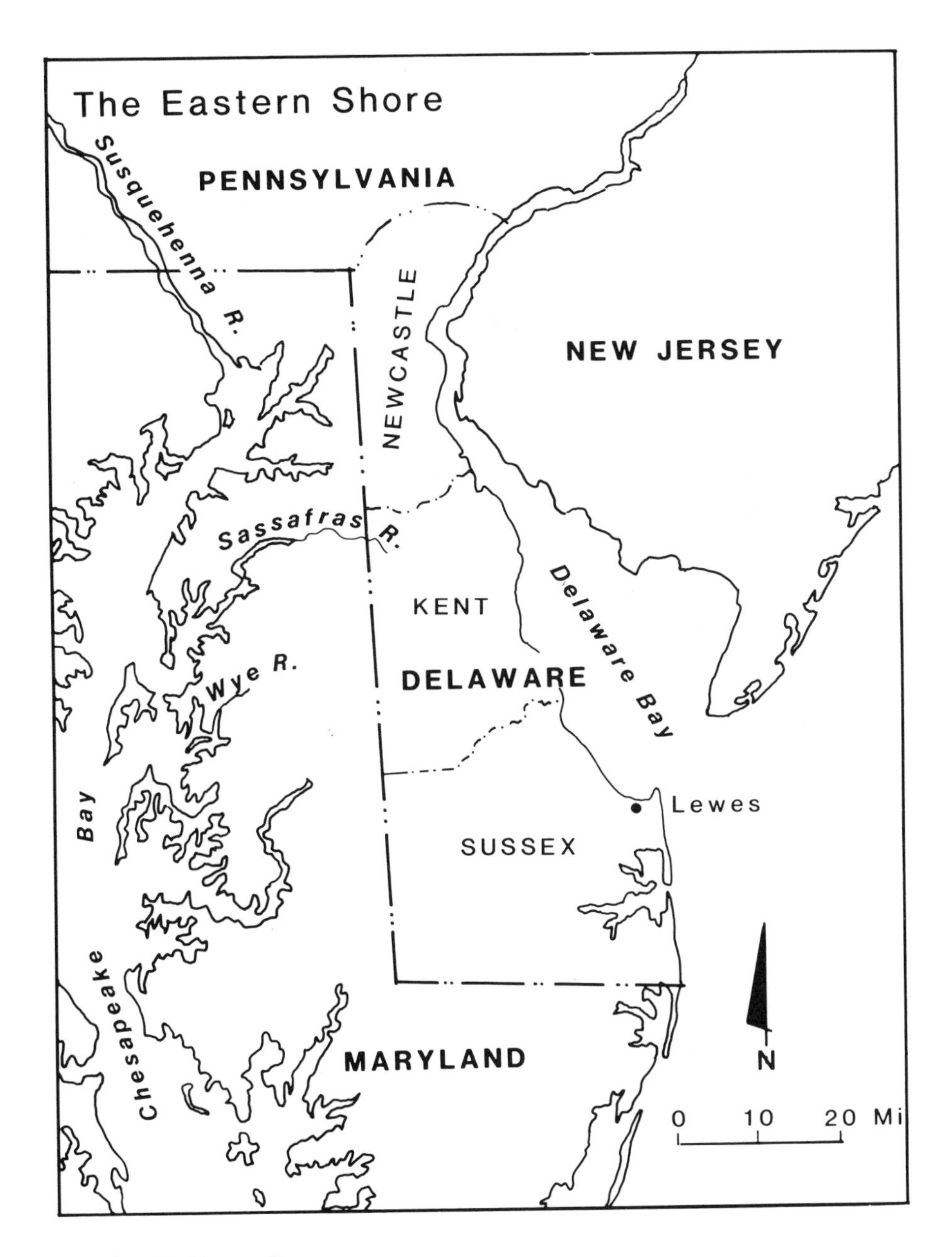

Map 4. The Eastern Shore.

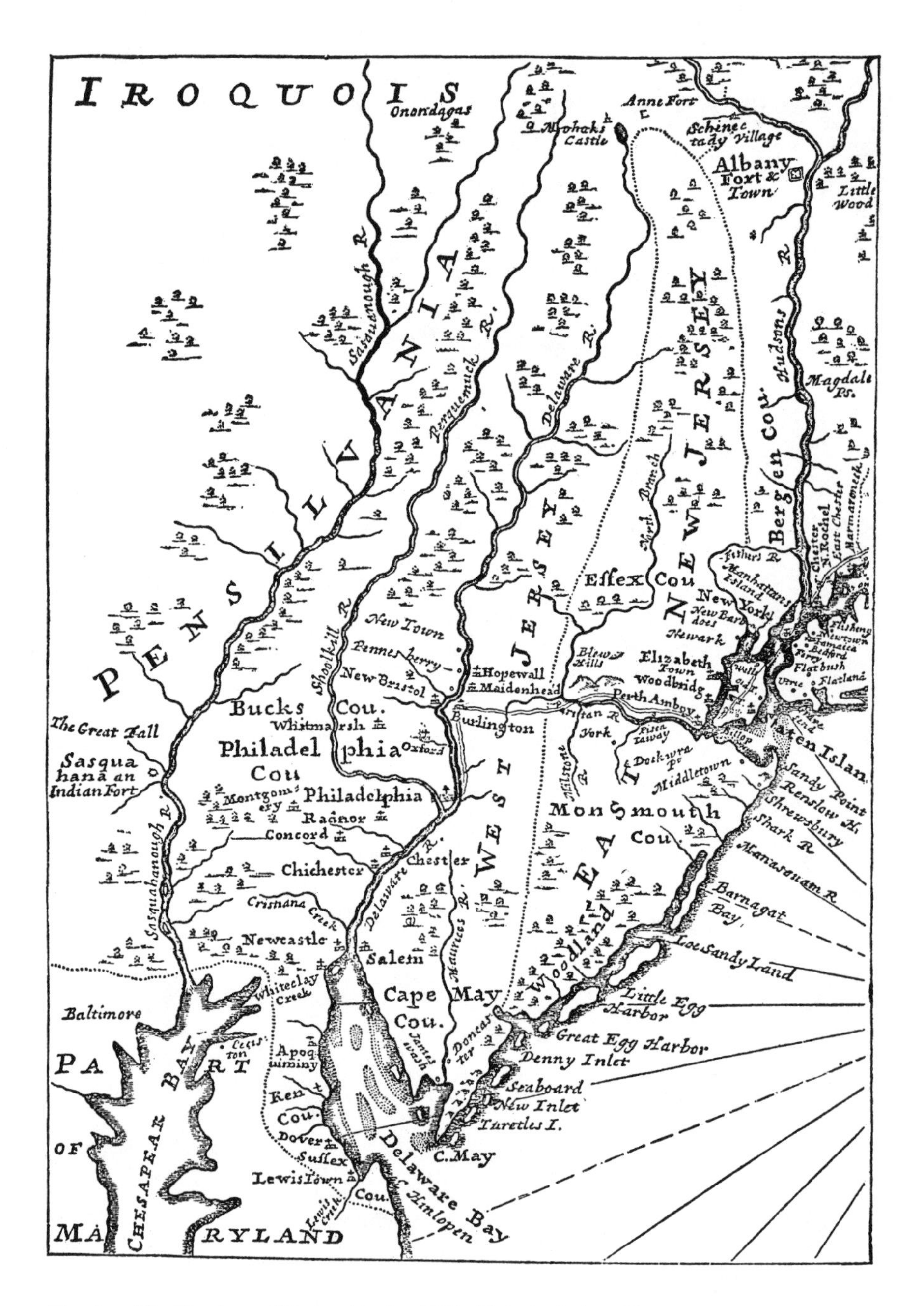

Map 5. The Province of Pennsylvania, 1730. This depiction, like many other maps drawn during this era, is somewhat inaccurate, which may account in part for Moraley's difficulty in finding his way through the countryside.

I afterwards carried Pipe Staves on my Shoulders, from the Land to the Ship, to the number of above thirty-six thousand. In a Fortnight after our Ship was loaded, when we had nothing else to do but to eat and drink, the Captain allowing us hot Meat Morning, Noon, and Night. But having about three Weeks on my Hands, I resolv'd to take a small Journey towards *Maryland*, and pass'd through the Counties of *Newcastle, Kent*, and *Sussex*. These are subject to the Province of *Pensilvania*, and are very unhealthy, being swampy Ground, and Fevers raging continually.

Newcastle is chief of the three Counties, the Assembly being kept there. *Lewes*, near the Sea, in *Sussex*, is a Fishing Town. I pass'd by *Bohemia Head* into *Maryland*, after I had crossed the Rivers *Susquehannah* and *Sassafras*, so call'd from abundance of those Trees growing along its Banks. Then *Wye* River, near which lived a Roman Catholick Gentleman, named *Richard Bennet*,[5] commonly call'd, *Poor Dick of Wye*, though the richest Man in those Parts. I soon after pass'd *Potomack* River, and went to Col. *Mason*,[6] a near Relation of my Mother's and was well receiv'd.[7] He invited me to stay; but fearing I should lose my Passage, I return'd back, he giving me six Pieces of Eight to bear my Expenses.

In a Wood near a Place call'd *Oppoquinomy*, I espied a Snake lying in a Path-way; and endeavouring to shun it by going out of the Road, I accidentally trod upon another, which immediately twisted itself about my Right Leg, and squeez'd it so hard, that I was afraid it would have broke. After I had stood some time, expecting to be bit, the Snake dropp'd upon the Ground, and I came off unhurt. I viewed it, and

5. Richard Bennet died in 1749 at age eighty-three at his seat in Queen Ann County. The local newspaper reported that he was "supposed to be the richest man in America." See Robert Barnes, *Marriages and Deaths from the Maryland Gazette, 1727–1839* (Baltimore: Genealogical Publishing Co., 1973), 11.

6. The primary residence of Colonel George Mason (1690–1735) was at Chickamuxon Creek, Charles County, Maryland, but Mason owned another estate across the Potomac River in Virginia. Because he was the third generation of Masons to live on the Chesapeake Bay, it is not clear how Moraley's mother, Martha Mason, could have been closely related, although it would not have been impossible. See Pamela C. Copeland and Richard K. MacMaster, *The Five George Masons: Patriots and Planters of Virginia and Maryland* (Charlottesville: University Press of Virginia, 1975), 56 and genealogical appendixes.

7. Moraley does not remember his route correctly. First, Lewes is far to the south, at the mouth of the Delaware Bay. Second, because the Susquehanna River drains into the northwest part of the Chesapeake Bay and the Sassafras and Wye rivers are on the eastern shore of the bay, Moraley could not have crossed all three in his journey south. Finally, the Potomac River separates Maryland and Virginia, so Moraley would have entered the latter colony if he crossed that river. Moraley may have visited Mason on the eastern shore of Maryland. Map 4 provides the correct geographic features of the eastern shore, while Map 5 shows a common but incorrect geographical understanding of the area in 1730.

found I had tread upon the Head, which prevented its Biting. I look'd upon this as a Mercy, and return'd Thanks to the Author of Good for my Deliverance. It was a Horn Snake, six Foot long.

The next Day I met a Woman, with two Children, walking the same Road. She had miss'd her Way, and desir'd me to direct her. I found she was bound to *Philadelphia*, and proffer'd to be assistant to her, upon Occasion, to carry her youngest Child, which was not three Years old, the other being about nine; and she in return bore my Charges. The second Day after we travell'd together, Night coming on, we were oblig'd to take our Lodging all Night under an Oak Tree, where you may depend I was not uncivil to her. It was in the Month of *August*; and the Weather being excessive warm, we were constrain'd to keep awake for fear of the Bears, which often roam about in the Night. In the Morning we proceeded towards *Bohemia Head*, and in two Days reach'd *Philadelphia*, where we parted.

From thence I went to *Burlington*, and repair'd to the Ship, when we had Notice to prepare for sailing in three Days. The Day being come, the Captain invited all his Friends on board, to take his Farewel of them; and I was order'd to clean my Kettles and Plates, and boil a Quarter of Mutton, and some Beef. The Company consisted of about 40 Persons. I serv'd up Dinner, receiv'd the Thanks of all present for my good Management, and the Punch Bowl going merrily about, I made a shift to get myself drunk before Three o'Clock. Whilst we were carousing, who should come to the Ship but the Woman I was speaking of before, and agreed with the Captain for her and her Children's Passage.

We stay'd four or five Days at *Philadelphia*, in order to take in more Provisions, during which Time I was frequently sent on Shore to fetch and carry Bottles for the Use of the Captain, when I was discovered by my Creditors, which put me into a Pannick Fear; but acquainting the Captain, he secured me close on board, where I guarded the Ship by myself, the Sailors being always on Shore taking their Leave of their Mistresses and Friends.

One Day as I was walking the Deck, a Boat came along Side of us, having a Gentleman in her, who desired Admittance. He was a handsome young *Irishman*, a Surgeon by Profession, but very much in Debt. I secured him in the Cabbin, but the next Morning he venturing upon Deck, the Water Bailiff[8] enter'd, seized and carried him to Jail for one Hundred and Forty Pounds.

8. The port authorities.

On the 26th of July, we sailed down [the] *Delaware*, and the next Day passed by *Chester*, Capital of the County of the same Name.[9] It is seated close to the River, and contains about two hundred Houses, adorn'd with pleasant Gardens and Orchards. There I was overtaken by my old Master *Edmund Lewis*, who demanded me of the Captain, on account of an Indenture between myself and him, but the Boat being in Haste, oblig'd him to step into her, otherwise he must have gone to Sea with us, the Ship being under Sail and so I escaped being carried back.

From hence we arrived at *Newcastle*, where we cast Anchor, and sent a Boat on Shore to buy more fresh Provisions. I was one and going to a House some Distance from the Town, we bought a Quarter of Mutton, and a Quarter of Beef. Myself and the Crew went into a Back Yard, where, with the help of a Stick and a Stone, we knocked down five Geese, and brought them on board, tying them by the Necks round our Waists, like *Aesop's* Goslings, to prevent their Cackling. After this Exploit we returned on board. *Newcastle* is a large Town, of about 400 Houses, neatly built, and inhabited by wealthy People.

The next Day, in the Morning, we perceived a lame Wild Goose swimming on the Surface of the Water, and a Bald Eagle attempting several times to seize her, which we prevented by shooting him, and sent a Boat, which took the Goose, of which we made a Sea Pye.

In the Afternoon a Boat came along the Ship's Side, and demanded to speak with the Captain, who came up, and they complained to him of the Loss of their Geese, and demanded Satisfaction. All Hands were called upon Deck, and the Captain asked every one of us, if we knew any thing concerning the Geese. We all stiffly denyed we had, or knew any thing about, them. So the Boat left us.

About Two in the Afternoon on the next Day, the Captain being upon Deck, with myself, the Geese being hungry, cackled. The Master hearing them, said to me, *How cou'd you have the Impudence to deny them*, and call'd up the Crew, and upbraided them with their Theft: But a brisk young Fellow boldly told him, that considering we had a long Voyage before us, and our Provisions but scanty, we thought we were obliged to take what lay in our Way, and wou'd pay for the Geese when we returned. The Captain laugh'd, and order'd me to kill one of them for Dinner. So I open'd the Forecastle, where I had stored my Firewood

9. The *Sea Flower*, commanded by Captain Oswald Peel, actually left Philadelphia during the week of September 19–26, 1734, according to the *Pennsylvania Gazette* published that week. The ship's destination was Dublin, Ireland. It had arrived in Philadelphia from Barbados on July 4.

and the Geese, and executed the Captain's Command, and roasted one of them for Dinner.

The next Day, the Wind proving favourable, we sailed down the River for the Capes, in two Days passed them, and in Two more sail'd above four hundred Miles; but the Wind shifting, we were obliged to lye by; a brisk Gale suddenly arising, we steer'd our Course towards *Ireland*; but an unlucky Mischance happen'd, for the Ship sprung a Leak, which obliged us to pump continually, changing Hands every half Hour, which harassed us to such a Degree, that if it had not been for God's Providence, we must have sunk under the Fatigue; but the Leak stopp'd by Pumping, and the Dirt on the Sides of the Ship getting into the Gap, we escaped. It was impossible to unload to find out the Defect, because we were full of Wood, wedg'd very close and hard.

We had in our Company the *Irish* Woman, a *Scotchman*, and an *Irishman*, named *Mullen*, who had three Wives, one at *Dublin*, one at *Philadelphia*, and one at *London*. Our Employment, during our Voyage, was diverting our selves with relating our Adventures; at other Times we washed our Linen. For my Part, I had but one Shirt to my back, and consequently had little Care on that account; so my chief Business was to endeavour to please the Company with my Cookery.

11 VOYAGE TO IRELAND—DUBLIN HARBOUR—ARRIVES AT WORKINGTON—"THE PICTURE OF ROBINSON CRUSOE"—"A GRAVE QUAKER"—MERRY MAKING—NETHER HALL—A TANKARD OF SUPERNACULUM—MR. SENHOUSE'S PLEASANTRIES—CROSBY.

THE Wind was not generally favourable to us, and we were eleven Weeks before we had any hopes of a Sight of the desir'd Port. But about 300 Miles, by the Computation of our Sailing, we discover'd a Ship, and made up to her. She prov'd a *Dublin* Ship from *Portugal.* The Captain agreed with us in our Reckning; but we out-sailing him, lost sight of them in the Night.

The next Day, I being under Deck, the Captain call'd me up to see a monstrous Whale, about two Miles from us, frisking upon the Waters, then diving down head foremost, and spouting Water from him. Afterwards we saw several large Birds, call'd *Gannets*, but by the *Scots* and *Irish, Solen Geese*; from which our Captain conjectur'd we were not far from Land. This prov'd true, for the next Day we got into Soundings, which we discover'd by our Plummets;[1] and in two Hours after saw the Western Coast of *Ireland*, near Cape *Clear*. We steer'd round the South-

1. The sailors discovered the sea bottom by dropping a piece of metal attached to a line.

ern Coast, and after we pass'd *Cork* and *Kingsale*, arriv'd in the Harbour of *Dublin*, after above thirteen Weeks Sail, and cast Anchor near *Rings-end*, not far from *Aston's Key*, from whence we discover'd the two Cathedrals, and had a Prospect of that famous City.

Here our Passengers left us; and the *Irishman* who had three Wives, skulk'd about Town for fear of his Wife. The *Irish* Woman I met in *America*, left us to go to her Father, who refus'd her Admittance to his House, bidding her go to her Husband in *Carolina*. For you must know, that about nine Years before her Arrival at *Dublin*, she had married an old Man, (by her Father's Orders, but entirely against her own Inclination) whose Effects lying at *Charles Town*, in *South Carolina*, they were forced to go thither; when she, repenting her Match, elop'd from him, and robb'd him of all his Household Furniture, which she sent by Sea to *Philadelphia*, herself and Children travelling it by Land on Foot.[2]

The Captain one Day coming on board, for he and the Men went every Day ashore, leaving me to stay by the Ship, I desir'd to be dismiss'd; but he told me, that as soon as he had sold the Cargo, he would carry me to *Whitehaven*, where he had a Mother and two Sisters living. But shortly after this, not disposing of his Goods, he was for sailing to *Carlingford*, about 36 Miles from *Dublin*, which disappointed me for the present.

About a Week after, there being a Collier[3] bound to *Workington*, in *Cumberland*, which was to sail the next Morning, I desired the Mate to dismiss me; to which he agreed, and sent four Hands with me in the Boat to the Ship, nam'd the *Leviathan*, Captain *Steel*, where I had a hearty Welcome from the generous Commander.

I observed the two Nights I was with him both Morning and Evening he read Prayers to the Crew. It was the only Ship I was ever in where there was no Swearing or prophane Talking. We set Sail at Seven

2. The mysterious Irish woman who robbed her husband and left him in Charles Town (Charleston) to return to Dublin could have been Mary Townsend. The following advertisement appeared in the Charleston newspaper on March 16, 1734: "Whereas a chaise, several parcels of linen, household goods, plate, and other things were lately stolen from my Plantation near the Quarter House and supposed to be concealed by some evil persons in and about Charlestown. A reward is offered for their discovery. All persons are cautioned against buying my cattle or other things from Mary Townsend, my now wife, as I will not allow receipt to be given by her and am not responsible for her debts.—J. Townsend." Other notices indicate that Joseph Townsend was involved in many local quarrels. See Alton T. Moran, *The South Carolina Gazette: Genealogical Abstracts, 1732–1735* (Bowie, Md.: Heritage Books, 1987), 64–65.

3. A coal-carrying vessel.

in the Morning with a constant fair Wind, and after seven Hours sailing, we passed by the *Isle of Man*, and reached *Workington*. The next Day, about eight in the Morning, a Custom Officer, named *Lowther*, boarded us, and, pitying my Condition, gave me a Note directed to Mr *Senhouse* of *Nether Hall*.[4] I got two Drams[5] before my Departure, took my Leave of the Ship, and set my foot upon *English* Ground, after three Years and eight Months Absence.

I was drest in the following Trim. I had a Shirt on above fourteen or fifteen Weeks, a miserable Pair of Breeches, adorn'd with many living Companions, two torn Waistcoats, no Coat, a coarse, lousy, Woolen Cap, an old Hat given me in *Ireland*, a Pair of torn Stockings, a bad Pair of Shoes supported by Packthread,[6] no Handkerchief: So I looked not unlike the Picture of *Robinson Crusoe*.

With these Disadvantages I was to travel about fourscore Miles before I reach'd *Newcastle*, through a Country where I was not known, and at the worst Time of the Year, it being the Day after *Christmas Day*, and so rainy, that for the nine Days I was trampousing home, there was scarce any Intermission, which very much discourag'd me; but making a Virtue of Necessity, I comforted myself with the Prospect of getting home, where I did not doubt of having the Fatted Calf kill'd for me.

I enter'd the Town of *Workington*, at that time very dirty, which being a Specimen of the Terribleness of the remaining Part of my Journey, I was uneasy, for I had not one Farthing[7] about me. So walking about the Town, musing on Ways and Means how I should get Intelligence of the right Road, a grave Quaker, sitting at his Door, ask'd me where I was bound. I readily acquiesc'd with his Demand, and he gave me Two-pence,[8] the first Money I had finger'd since I left *America*.

So leaving him, I repair'd to *Workington Hall*, the Seat of the *Curwens*; but not meeting with Encouragement, I remember'd Mr *Lowther's* Note to Mr *Senhouse*, and endeavour'd to inform myself of his Abode. So leaving this dirty Town, I met with two Gentleman's Servants, who told me they were going a merry making, and said if I would accompany them, they would direct me in the Road to *Nether Hall*. I readily

4. Humphrey Senhouse of Netherhall, Cumberland, is mentioned briefly in Stephen and Lee, *Dictionary of National Biography*, 17:1182.

5. A "dram" is a small draught of alcohol.

6. A stout thread or twine often used for tying bundles.

7. One-fourth of a pence.

8. Twelve pence equaled one shilling.

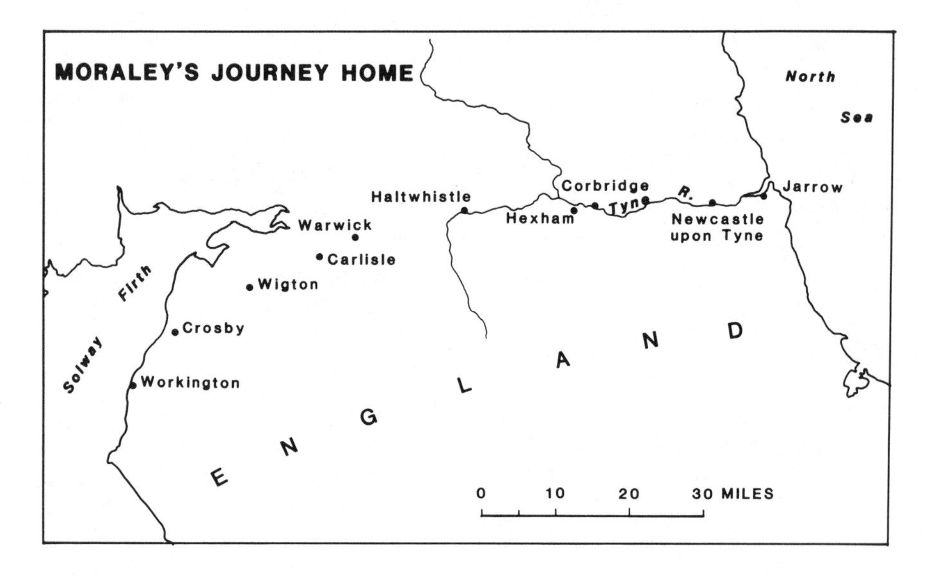

Map 6. Moraley's journey home.

agreed to follow them, hoping by their means I should have an Opportunity to exercise my Grinders, being hungry; and my Desire was accomplish'd, for we had not travell'd long before an Alehouse presented itself to our View, when I gladly heard them propose to bait.[9] So we enter'd the House, where we drank two Quarts of Ale, and I being sharp set, desir'd something to eat. Accordingly a Plate of Goose Pye was brought, which I soon dispatch'd.

The Reckning being paid, we proceeded forward, when one of the Persons looking steadfastly at me, said he knew me, and then told me he was one of those who carried my Mother and Mr *Brown* in a Boat to *Jarrow*, to be married.[10] This I was a Stranger to, as to Mr *Brown's* Marriage with her; tho' I knew at *Philadelphia* she was married to a

9. To eat.

10. Moraley's mother, Martha Isaacson, wed for the third time to Thomas Brown on September 25, 1732, at South Shields, a town east of Jarrow and also on the south side of the Tyne River (IGI). The marriage bond taken out on August 9, 1732, lists Thomas Brown of Newcastle as an armiger—that is, a man entitled to armorial bearings, a gentleman or squire; his co-signer on the bond, Matthew Dawson, was also a gentleman (*Durham Marriage Bonds, 1730–1738* [Microfilm, Family History Library, Salt Lake City, British Film Area #1040263], 63). The former Martha Mason, who had inherited some valuable property from her first husband, seems to have consistently improved her social standing through marriage, advancing from wife of a watchmaker to wife of a Captain and then of a gentleman.

Justice of the Peace, which in some measure occasion'd me to come home.

Parting from these two Men, I travell'd I know not where, to find out *Nether Hall*; but not meeting with any body to give me Information, I rambled till it began to grow Dark; when, as good Luck would have it, I discovered a new House, which I made up to, and perceiving a good-look'd Man, he invited me in, gave me two Pints of good Ale, and directed me to *Nether Hall*. So steering from thence, after much Difficulty, through Dirt and Water, I discover'd an old Castle at a good Distance, and made up to it; but several Water Places intervening, I was obliged to wade through them, up to the Waist, before I could get to the Castle, when I discovered a Light.

After passing a small Bridge, before a Garden adorn'd with Leaden Images, I enter'd the Kitchen, wherein were an old Lady turning a Beef Stake with a Pair of Beef Tongs, attended by the Household Steward and his Wife, a good pretty Woman, and House-keeper to the Family. Upon my first approach, I asked for Mr *Senhouse*, and, stepping forward, the Lady asked me from whence I came, and where bound; which having answered to effect, she demanded what Trade I followed: To which I answer'd, Clock and Watch-making was my Business. Says she, You look more like a Chimney Sweeper. Madam, answer'd I, it is no Wonder, I should make such an Appearance, considering the Hardships I have undergone in my Voyage.

She was going on when Mr *Senhouse* came down Stairs into the Kitchen, and demanded my Business; so producing my Credentials from Mr *Lowther*, he bad me sit down. Then surveying my external Edifice, he asked where I intended to lye that Night. I answer'd, Where God's good Providence directed me. Well, said he, for that Expression you shall not be exposed to the Inclemency of the Weather: I will provide for you To-night, and To-morrow will give you such Security, as will carry you home.

Then he ask'd me, if I knew any Body at *Newcastle*. To which I answer'd, I knew almost every Body. He said, Do you know the Recorder?[11] Yes, Sir, said I, I have Reason to know him. Why, who is he? What is his Name, says he? To which I replyed, His Name is *Isaacson*; his Brother, Capt. *Charles Isaacson*, married my Mother. Thus making myself known, had a good Effect; for he, in the first Place, order'd a brown Toast, and a Tankard of *Supernaculum*, to be given me. Then

11. Magistrate or judge.

order'd his Steward to get me some Necessaries. The Steward brought me an old Coat, about half a Yard too long for me, an old Wig, an old Pair of Hose, and a good Shirt worth about Ten Shillings. The Footman was ordered to shave me, which he did, and bereaved me of a troublesome Companion in so doing, for he had been my Chum for above 14 Weeks.

Mr *Senhouse* coming in soon after I was renovated, asked me pleasantly which of his Maids I liked best. To which I replyed, They were so agreeable, that I could not prefer the one to the other. After some merry Discourse had pass'd, I went to Bed, and sleep'd for the first Time in a Bed since I had left *Philadelphia*. In the Morning the Servant awaked me, and said his Master desired me to come to him. He was in the Kitchen waiting for me, when he gave me four Half Crowns,[12] and a recommendatory Letter to divers Gentlemen on the Road. And told me, He expected me to write to him when I got home, otherwise he should not think I was the same Person I said I was.

After promising him that I would write to him when I arrived at *Newcastle*, I proceeded towards a little Town near the Sea, called *Crosby*. At my first Enterance, I perceived a Parson smoaking a Pipe; by his Appearance he seemed the Curate.[13] He accosted me in a civil Manner, and invited me to his House, which was a neat Place, indifferently furnished; the best of his Goods being a handsome brown Wife, dress'd in a clean brown Gown, and a blue Topknot. Here I drank two Pints of his good Ale, and smoaked a Pipe. It is a hundred to one if the Vicar[14] would have regaled me so well; for Men in plentiful Circumstances, seldom or never consider the Wants of the Needy.

He directed me to one *Harriman*, a Clock-maker, living at the Upper-end of the Town, who was very civil to me, and invited me to stay with him two or three Days, till I had recovered the Fatigues of my Voyage, which I did, and assisted him in two or three Jobs in my Way, and departed from him towards *Tallontire Hall*, the Seat of Mr *Partis*, where I arrived about Eleven in the Morning, and enter'd the Kitchen, where Mrs *Partis* was making White Puddings.[15] Upon my making myself known, she caused to be brought in a Quart of as good Beer as ever I drank in my Life, and I eat the best Part of the Ribs of a Quarter of Lamb.

12. A half crown was the equivalent of 2 shillings and 6 pence.

13. A clergyman who acts in the capacity of a deputy or assistant.

14. A parish priest who receives a stipend.

15. Part of the stomach or entrails of an animal stuffed with a mixture of minced meat, oatmeal, seasoning, and other assorted items.

12 SIR RICHARD MUSGRAVE—HALTWHISTLE—BELATED IN A FELL—CORBRIDGE, WYLAM, ETC.—ARRIVES IN NEWCASTLE.

THEN leaving her, I marched towards *Hayton Castle*, the Seat of the late Sir *Richard Musgrave*, Bar[one]t and on *Saturday* in the Evening reached the Town; when hearing the Tooting of a Bag-pipe, I fancied it was an Ale-house, and was not deceived in my Conjecture. The first Thing I said here was, If I could have a Lodging. The Landlady said, Have you any Money? Yes, said I, and put a half Crown between my Teeth. Sir, says the old Bedlam,[1] you are welcome; will you have any Thing to eat. To which I answer'd, With all my Heart. She set before me a Plate charged with Goose Pye; the Intelects were good enough, but the external Frame was as brown as the Parson's Wife's Face, spoken of before.

After I had finished my Meal, a Man in the Chimney Corner called me by Name, and desired me to do as he did: There were three Men

1. "Bedlam" is a term for a person suited for a lunatic asylum, although Moraley may have meant "beldam," a common eighteenth-century pejorative term meaning an old woman.

with him, they drank Brandy and Ale, to the Tune of four Quarts, which made me so merry, that I danced with the Piper.[2] Afterwards the Company paid their Reckoning and departed, and I went to Bed. The next Morning I drank a Quart of Ale, paid for it, and proceeded to the Castle of Sir *Richard Musgrave*. In the Kitchen were Three or Four of his Servants, who I begg'd to tell their Master I desired to speak with him. He appeared, and ordered me a Horn of Drink,[3] which was given me, with Three Shillings.

Then I pass'd through a Road between *Hayton* and *Sparetree*, and baited at the Sign of the *Blue Anchor*, which was occupied by a handsome young Landlady, who gave me some Goose Pye, and two Pots of Ale. From thence, about Eleven, I arriv'd at *Sparetree*, a pitiful dirty Hole, having a Church. Passing thro', I perceiv'd a Coach with a Gentleman in it, which was our Collector *Lawson's* Son, preceded by the Family Steward,[4] who with a surly Tone ask'd me where I was bound. But I not regarding him nor his Demand, went directly to *Brighton Hall*, the Seat of *Gilfred Lawson*, Esq; who was walking in his Kitchen Garden, in a *Scotch* Plad Night Gown. He very civily ask'd me where I was going; which having resolv'd, he order'd me two Horns of Ale, and a new Three Half-penny Brick,[5] with some Potted Beef, and gave me two Shillings. Afterwards he gave me another Shilling, and directed me to *Wigton*, about seven Miles from his House.

Here, after four Hours Travel, over Hills and Dales, thro' Rain and Dirt, I discover'd the Church when almost dark and enter'd the Town, a small Place, and every other House in it an Ale-house; so, consequently, they have no Trade but on the Market days. I quarter'd at the *George*; but having considered I had a long Journey home, I got up the next Morning by Four o'Clock, taking my Route to *Carlisle*, which I reach'd at Three that Afternoon, and took up my Residence at the *Royal Oak*. Here I got acquainted with a Watch-maker, and did a Job, for which I got a Shilling and a good Drink, and retir'd to my Quarters, where the civil Landlord gave me some Goose Pye, and some frigacied Rabbit.

In the Morning I survey'd the City, which I believe is the least in *England*, but surrounded by a very strong Wall. The Houses are very handsome, being fronted with smooth Stone, and the Streets very clean.

2. A colloquialism meaning that Moraley got drunk.
3. A draught of ale or some other alcohol.
4. An official who controlled the domestic affairs of the household.
5. A loaf of bread in the shape of a brick.

Leaving *Carlisle*, I directed my Course next towards *Corby Castle*, the Seat of a Gentleman nam'd *Howard*. In the Midway lies a Town belonging to the Earl of *Carlisle*, called *Torkat*, I lodg'd there all Night at an Ale-house, and had to Supper Goose Pye and hot Rice Milk. In the Morning, about Eleven or Twelve o'Clock, I discover'd *Corby Castle*, seated near the Banks of the River *Eden*. Adjoining to it are several Fields with many Relicks of Religious Worship, and in an Out Building an exceeding fine Chapel, the Altar adorn'd with several curious Ornaments.

I afterwards went into the Kitchen, where by the Fire-side, I saw all Sorts of the best Delicacies, such as Ducks, Geese, Pies, Puddings, Chickens, Jellies; in short, they put me in mind of the old *English* Hospitality. A young Lady, Daughter to Mr *Howard*, appear'd, and ask'd my Business; to which I answer'd, that being distress'd by Shipwreck, I was necessitated to ask Charity of well disposed Christians. She immediately went to her Father, who sent me Half a Crown.

But the Lady calling out for Mr *Ridley*, the Butler, to bring in more Wine, I took the Opportunity of changing my Name; and the Butler discharging his Duty, came back, and ask'd me my Name, which I said was *Ridley*. He hearing this, ask'd me of what Family I deriv'd my Pedigree; to which I reply'd, from *Willemoteswick*, and deduced my Descent from these Marriages spoken of before. I likewise told him, that being of the *Romish* Religion, my Parents discarded me, which oblig'd me to seek my Fortune. The Design taking, he gave me a Half Crown, and two Glasses of White Wine; so I left him to chew on the Cud, and departed.

The next Place I visited was *Warwick Hall*, the Seat of a Family so call'd; but the Gentleman being abroad, I was disappointed, and went towards *Haltwhistle*, and pass'd over *Coal Fell*, a dismal Place, where I met with no one Person to inform me how to proceed. This barren Place put me in mind of Mount *Atlas* and *Causacus*; for look which Way you will, you shall see nothing but Hill over Hill. After three Hours I discover'd *Haltwhistle*, and arrived at a little lone House near the Boundaries of the two Counties, where I was known, and treated with Goose Pye, and Wheaten Bannock[6] and Milk.

From thence I went to *Haltwhistle*, and quarter'd at *Barbara Bell's*, and the next Morning went to *Crow Hall*, formerly the Seat of the *Ridleys*, where I was known; from which I had a Sight of *Willemoteswick*

6. A type of bread.

Castle. I left *Crow Hall*, and pass'd over *Hayton Bridge*, and so towards *Hexham*; but about two Miles from it, I was belated, and lost in a Fell. It rain'd, and the Wind blew terribly hard. Here I thought my Condition was as bad as in *America*; but I soon discovered an old House, which I made up to, and desir'd Admittance. The People observing the Badness of my Attire did not readily comply with my Request; but a Man asking my Name, which having told him, he said he would admit me, because he had once a friend of that Name, whom I soon persuaded him was my Father's Brother. I had some Milk and Bread for Supper, but for a Bed I was obliged to lye with the Cows in the Byer[7] under the House, upon a little Straw, and with a shabby Coverlid.[8]

In the Morning he rous'd me up, and conducted me through a Wood, opposite to *Sandhoe*, to *Hexham*, where I left him, and enquir'd for Mr *John Ridley*, Brother to the Chief of that Family. He liv'd at *Battle Hill*. I knock'd at the Door, which his Wife open'd, and I ask'd, If her Husband was at home? Her Answer was, What Business have you with him! Tell him, Madam, said I, I am a Relation to him. You a Relation to him! said she, and so shut to the Door, and I was forced to trudge forward on my Journey.

From thence I pass'd over *Corbridge*, and baited at the *Golden Angel*; then went through *Ovingham*, then *Wylam*, and at length got to *Newburn*, where my Feet began to bleed: But remembering I had an old Friend, Mrs *Capstack*, I met with a handsome Reception; and so march'd towards home. I was ever looking for St *Nicolas* Church Steeple with the greatest Impatience, but did not discover till I came to the *Quarry House*. So passing by my Father's House, it being shut up, I went to Mr *Moraley's*, who lived then in the *Bigg-market*, where I met with a very kind Reception, and continued there three Weeks; after which I liv'd with my Mother till her Death, which happen'd about three Years and some Months after. Since that time I have experienc'd the greatest Misfortune, occasion'd by the Mistake of her Executors,[9] which is briefly as follows.

7. A "byre" is a cow-house or shed.

8. A covering of any kind.

9. The persons appointed by Moraley's mother to execute her will. The wills of Moraley's parents are reprinted in Appendix C.

POSTSCRIPT: THE AUTHOR'S CASE, RECOMMENDED TO THE GENTLEMEN OF THE LAW.

MY Mother had made a Will, and the Persons she appointed her Executors, seiz'd her Effects and Freehold, without an Administration granted them, and in conformity to her Will; of which they denied me a Copy, sold the Personal Effects, and refus'd to give me an Inventory of them. I endeavour'd to persuade them my Father's Will was never prov'd by her, and a Letter from *London* was produc'd to make my Assertion good, but all in vain. I was advis'd to have a Monition read at St *John's* Church, which was done, but the Executors never appear'd; tho' to prevent my Plea, which was *Bona Notabilia*, they procured Administration by unfair Practices, for which they charg'd me £4. An eminent Attorney procur'd a Copy of my Father's Will, and made it appear my Mother was only Tenant for Life, by the Custom of the City of *London*, tho' she mortgaged it for Fifty Pound, without my Knowledge.

If a Father is a Freeman of London, he cannot devise the Disposition of the Body of Infant, by the Statute of 12 Car. II &c. if he do, yet the Infant shall remain in the Custody of the Mayor and Aldermen; and this Custom, to have the Custody of the Orphans Person, of his Real and Personal Estate, extends to Lands out of London, SID. 363. —And, *The Children of a Freeman may exhibit a Bill in the Lord Mayor's Court of Equity, having a Discovery of their Father's Estate, and for the Recovery of their Part, by the Custom of* London.[1]

I soon after seiz'd the Freehold; but the Executor procured a Warrant from a Justice of the Peace to shew cause why I shou'd not be imprison'd for dispossessing them; but I was released upon a Promise given, that I would not disturb them. I dispossessed them again; then Ejectments were served both against me and them, and the Executors told me, the Mortgagee was upon prosecuting them for not making Payment out of the personal Goods. Upon which I agreed to make a Sale of the House, purely to make them easy, by preventing a Law Suit.

But first we had a Meeting, in order to settle the Accounts of the Money arising from the Sale of Goods, when the Executors produced the Sum Total, which was Two Hundred and Six Pound; but afterwards they produced another of Seventy Three Pound short of the First; since which, I could never obtain either of the former Accounts. I was told, if I would release them, they would deliver me the remaining Effects, which I did, but have never received those Effects.

I was after this arrested for a small Debt, and in Custody of a Serjeant, but delivered by the Assistance of two Gentlemen, who paid the Charges. I afterwards convey'd the Freehold for One Hundred and Sixty Pound, which cost Five Hundred and Ten Pound, out of which I paid in my own Wrong Eighty-one Pound, and received only Seventy-nine Pound. At the Conveyance I demanded the Mortgage Deed and Security to be delivered up, but was refused, and threatened, by a Person present, if I did not immediately make a Conveyance, he would arrest me for the Debt I owed him. The Fear of a Prison, rather than any other Consideration, compelled me to the Sale.

Having paid all my Debts with the Money received, the Remainder was very inconsiderable; so that I am obliged at present to follow the meanest Imploy for a Subsistance, and shall endeavour to perswade the World to have a better Opinion of me than to think, that any Necessity shall compel me to act any otherwise than what is consistent with my Duty to God and my Neighbour; being sensible, whatever Hardships I

1. Appendix C explains the legal matters concerning Moraley's inheritance and reproduces the wills of his father and mother.

may lie under in this Life, tho' ever so afflicting, that they are infinitely preferrable to an Estate got by illegal Means; for tho' ill Persons may and do thrive for a While; yet a Time will come that will bring to light the hidden Things of Darkness,[2] when every one will be rewarded according to his Works.

I shall also endeavour, by my future Conduct, to make my Life easy under my unhappy Circumstance, by an entire Resignation to the Will of Providence, who has supported me thro' so many dangerous and tempestuous Seas of Adversity, and brought me safe to Land, where I continue, by the generous Assistance of the humane Inhabitants, a living Monument of God's Mercy.

FINIS.

2. 1 Corinthians 4:5–6: "Therefore judge nothing before the time, until the Lord come, who both will bring to light the hidden things of darkness, and will make manifest the counsels of the hearts: and then shall every man have praise of God. . . . Learn in us not to think of men above that which is written, that no one of you be puffed up for one against another."

Appendixes

APPENDIX A: THE BOOK AND ITS AUTHOR

John White first printed Moraley's autobiography, probably at the author's own expense, in 1743 at Newcastle-upon-Tyne, England. The William L. Clements Library at the University of Michigan currently holds a copy of that edition, a photocopy of which provided the basis for the version reproduced here. John Wilson, a friend of the Moraley family, first purchased the Clements Library copy of the *Infortunate*. Subsequently, he sold his copy to Thomas Bell, who wrote a brief history of the volume based on an interview with Wilson:

> The following exceedingly rare publication was printed in Newcastle, by White, in 1743. [I]t was purchased at the Sale of the Library of the late Mr. John Rawling Wilson, who esteemed it, a work of the greatest rarity, and one, on which he set an uncommon Value. [N]ot only on account of its scarcity, but from an Interest he had felt in the Narrative, when a Child; Moraley having been known to, and esteemed by his parents; and in a Conversation I had with Wilson respecting him & this Work, he (Wilson) told me that the Narrative was undoubtedly true; that Moraley was of a highly respectable Family, but a spend-thrift;—and who, on his settling in Newcastle, contrived to make a livelihood as a Watch-maker, tho' an easy,

> and good natured fellow, whose wants were few, and cares, less.—He died in January 1762 and was buried in St Nicholas ChurchYard.[1]

Bell also recounted his understanding of Moraley's life for the Newcastle local antiquarian, M. A. Richardson:

> January 19. [1762]—Buried, "William Morley, Watchmaker," (*St. Nicholas' Register*.) This singular individual, whose real name was Moraley, was of good family and the heir to a considerable paternal estate,[2] which was spent in reckless extravagance and eventually he had to make a living as a watchmaker in Newcastle: —He published in 1743, an account of various transactions which had occurred to himself, previous to that year, under the title of "The Unfortunate: or, the Voyage and Adventures of William Moraley of Moraley in Northumberland, Gent." The late Mr. J. R. Wilson, had a copy of this extremely scarce tract, which at his sale, was purchased by Mr. Thomas Bell, land-surveyor, a work abounding in extraordinary and romantic incidents, but which is understood to have been a faithful record of the circumstances of his early life.[3]

Bell's heirs sold the book to the Clements Library in 1925.[4] In 1884 the *Delaware County Republican* (Chester, Pa.) published the *Infortunate* in an abridged and expurgated version. This was an exact copy of a contemporary reprinting of the autobiography in the *Newcastle Chronicle*, which had divided the volume into chapters and had added chapter summaries. Copies of this truncated version survive at the New York Public Library and at the Historical Society of Pennsylvania, Philadelphia.

1. Manuscript sheet tipped into the University of Michigan William L. Clements Library copy of Moraley's autobiography and attributed to Thomas Bell. A copy of the book in the Newcastle Central Library contains the same information written in a different hand at the front of the volume. Another manuscript note in the Newcastle Library copy identifies this as a second, expanded edition of Moraley's memoirs. If true, no trace of an earlier version can be found.

2. This is inaccurate, because Moraley's father left young William a bequest of only 20 shillings and some watchmaker's tools. Bell may have meant that Moraley was heir apparent to a considerable fortune—which, in fact, he never received.

3. M. A. Richardson, *The Local Historian's Table Book, of Remarkable Occurrences, Historical Facts, Traditions, Legendary and Descriptive Ballads, etc., etc., Connected with the Counties of Newcastle-upon-Tyne, Northumberland and Durham*, 8 vols. (Newcastle-upon-Tyne: Richardson, 1841), 2 (pt. 1): 104.

4. B. D. Maggs and E. U. Maggs, *Bibliotheca Americana et Philippina*, pt. 4, no. 465 (London, 1925), 193.

APPENDIX B: MORALEY GENEALOGY

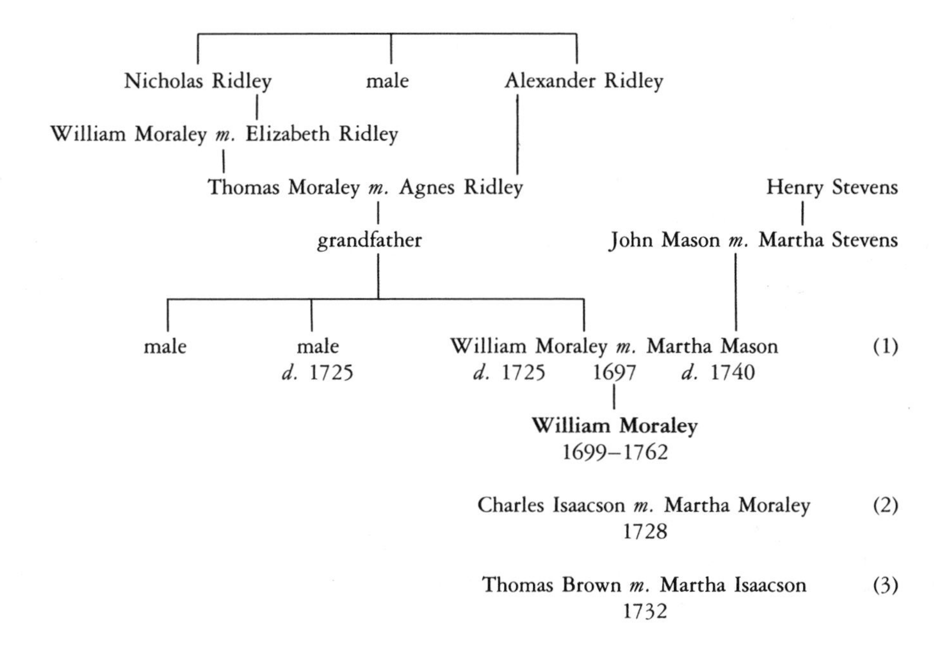

Note: All years have been converted to the new-style calendar, so William Moraley's birth, for example, is given here as 1699, although it was recorded as 1698. William Moraley was born February 25, 1699; baptized on March 1, 1699, at Christ Church, Greyfriars, Newgate; and buried on January 19, 1762, at St. Nicholas Church, Newcastle.

(1) William Moraley married Martha Mason on November 24, 1697, by virtue of a license from the Office of the Archbishop of Canterbury, London.

(2) Martha Moraley married Captain Charles Isaacson on October 19, 1728, at St. Andrew's, Newcastle.

(3) Martha Isaacson married Thomas Brown, armiger, on September 25, 1732, at South Shields, Durham.

APPENDIX C: THE WILLS OF WILLIAM MORALEY'S PARENTS

Moraley's arguments in the Postscript (pp. 141–43) oversimplify the legal questions concerning the testamentary provision of his parents' wills. Contrary to his assertions, the wills of both of his parents were properly proven, in timely fashion, in the Consistory Court of the Archbishop of Durham, the appropriate jurisdiction for Newcastle. His mother's executors sold her effects, as mandated by her will, to purchase annuities for Moraley's support. The executors posted a £50 bond with the court to carry out the will of Martha Mason Moraley Isaacson Brown. The legal theory put forward by Moraley and his attorney was that his father's estate should have been probated in the Lord Mayor's Court in London because his father, as a member of the Clockmakers Company, was a freeman of London. This court was a court of equity, and it had the authority to overturn the specific provisions of the will and to order that one-third of the estate be provided for the support of the children of the descendant—that is, given to William Moraley. If his father's will were invalidated and the provisions of the intestate laws invoked, then his mother's will likewise would be nullified because she would have had no right to the entire property. Instead, she would have held the balance of the property as a tenant for life and consequently would have been barred from directing the disposal of her former husband's estate. In any event, the arguments became moot when Moraley forcibly seized the house, ejected the executors, and then agreed to the sale of the house to avoid both a lawsuit and imprisonment. His behavior at this juncture is puzzling, even irrational. Perhaps the pent-up frustration of forty-one years as a dependent—combined with the provisions of his mother's will, which would have kept him in dependency for the rest of his life—produced the events described in the final pages of his autobiography.[1]

Following are the wills of William Moraley's father and mother, currently located in the Archives of the Consistory Court of the Archbishop of Durham, Division of Archives and Special Collections, University Library, University of Durham, England. We have silently added punctuation. William Moraley did not leave a will at his own death in 1762.

Will of William Moraley's Father, Probated 1725

Know all men by these presents that I, William Moraley of the Towne of Newcastle upon Tyne in the County of Northumberland, Watch maker, in perfect health and Memory doth make my Last Will and Testament in Manner and forme following: that is to say when all my Debts and funerall charges is satisfied, which shall be with the Least Expence that can be—I give all my Estate both Reall and Personell unto My Dear and Beloved Wife Martha Moralay. Excepting my Working tools and twenty shilling in money which I give unto my Son William Moraley in order to gett his Living. [A]nd more over, by virtue of these presents, I doe Appoint my said Loving Martha Moraley My whole and sole Executrix of this my Last will and testament; as witness My hand and Seal the Eleventh day of November in the year of our Lord one thousand seven hundred and twenty five.

William Moraley

Signed Sealled & Published by Wm Morraley
as & for his last will & Testam[en]t in our presence
who in presence of the s[ai]d Wm Morraley
subscribed our names as wittnesses
thereunto
Ja[mes] Bell
Tho[ma]s Armstrong
Char[les] Smithson
15. Martii 1725/6

1. We are indebted to Dr. J. M. Fewster, Senior Assistant Keeper, and Mrs. J. L. Drury, Assistant Keeper, of the Division of Archives and Special Collections of the University of Durham Library for their generous assistance in tracing and explaining the wills and court procedures.

Jurat fuer[un]t supranol[m]i[n]ata
Martha Moraley Vidua et Executrix
ac Jacobus Bell Testis
coram me
Ed: Bell Sur[rogate]:

Will of William Moraley's Mother, Probated 1740

In the Name of God, Amen. I, Martha Brown of the Town and County of Newcastle upon Tyne, Widdow, being infirm in Body but of Sound Perfect and disposeing Mind and Memory, Do think fit to make this my last Will and Testament in manner and form following. First, I Comitt my Soul to God who gave it, hopeing for the Pardon of all my Sins through the Meritts and Satisfaction of my Blessed Saviour, and my body to the Earth to be decently buryed according to the discretion of my Executors hereafter Named. Next, I order and Appoint all my Just Debts and funerall Expences to be fully satisfyed and paid. Item, I Do hereby Give, Devise and bequeath unto James Bell of the Town and County of Newcastle upon Tyne, Gentleman, Timothy Forster of Newcastle aforesaid, Surgeon, and Thomas Watson of Newcastle aforesaid, Gentleman, And to their Heirs, Executors, Administrators and assigns All my Messuage, Tenement or dwelling house Wherein I now live and Garden thereunto adjoyning, together with All and Singular the rights, Members and Appurtenances thereunto belonging; scituate, Standing, lying, and being, at or Near a certaine place called the Firth, and also all my household Goods and Furniture, Plate, Rings, Watches and Personall Estate of what nature or kind soever, which I shall be possessed of at the time of my Death upon Special Trust and Confidence and to and for the Uses, Intents and purposes hereafter Mentioned: (that is to say) Upon Trust that they, the said James Bell, Timothy Forster and Thomas Watson, their Heirs, Executors, Administrators and Assigns, Shall and do, so soon as Conveniently may be after my decease, Sell, Convey and Dispose of all my said Messuage, Tenement or Dwelling house, Garden and personall Estate for the best price that cann be gotten for the Same; and after the said premises shall be so Sold shall and do so soon as they conveniently can, lay out and Expend all such Sume and Sumes of Money that shall arise by such sale after payment of my Debts and funerall Expences in the purchaseing one or more Annuity or Annuities in Money to be secured and made payable out of Lands, or by other good Security, to the said James Bell, Timothy Forster and Thomas Watson, their Heirs, Executors, Administrators and Assigns, as they the said James Bell, Timothy Forster and Thomas Watson, their Heirs, Executors, Administrators and Assigns shall approve of, for and dureing and unto the full end and Term of the Naturall Life of my beloved Son William Morley. And after the receiveing such Annuity or Annuities shall and do Devide and pay the same in eaqual Monthly Shares and Proportions, Yearly and ever Year, to my said Son, William Morley, for and dureing his Naturall Life; first deducting all such Charges and Expences As they the said James Bell, Timothy Forster and Thomas Watson, their Executors, Administrators, Heirs and Assigns shall Expend or be put to in the Execution and performance of the aforesaid Trust or any way relateing thereunto. Nevertheless, it is my Mind and Will and I Do order and Appoint that it shall and may be lawfull to and for the said James Bell, Timothy Forster and Thomas Watson, their Heirs, Executors, Administrators and Assigns untill such Annuity or Annuities shall be purchased as aforesaid to pay to my said Son out of the Sume or Sumes of Money ariseing by sale of my said reall or personall Estates or the Rents and profits such Weakly allowance or Maintenance as they shall think Necessary and Convenient.

Item, I give and bequeath unto my Sister Elizabeth Owton My best blew Silk damask Suit, My Green Tabby Suit of Cloths, and my White Night Gown together with the one halfe of my Body or wearing Linnen.

Item, I give and bequeath to my Servant Ann Kirkhouse All my other wearing Apparell, Cloths and Body or wearing Linnen. Item, I do hereby Name, Constitute and Appoint the said James Bell, Timothy Forster and Thomas Watson, Joynt Executors of this My Last Will and Testament, Revokeing and makeing Void All former and other Wills whatsoever by me at any time heretofore made. In Witness whereof I have hereunto sett my Hand and Seal this Twelvth day of November in the Twelvth Year of the Reign of our Soveraign Lord King George the second over Great Brittaine, France and Ireland and so forth, And in the Year of our Lord One thousand seven hundred thirty and Eight.

Martha Brown

Signed Sealed Published and Declared by the above Martha Brown for and as her last Will and Testament in the presence of us who in the presence and at the request of the above named Testatrix have hereunto suscribed our Names as Witnesses to the Executeing thereof

Henry Isaacson
John Airey
Mark Ogle

December the 17th 1740. Henry Isaacson a Subscribing Witness—was sworn to the due Execution hereof and Timothy Forster—One of the Executors herein nam'd was also Sworn well & truly—to Execute & perform &c

before me
Tho[mas] Maddison
Surrogate

APPENDIX D: MORALEY AS A LITERARY ARTISAN

William Moraley's autobiography is suggestive about the reading habits of the English "middling sort" during the early eighteenth century. In it, Moraley alludes to a number of books, including Aesop's fables, the Bible, Dr. John Tillotson's "Rule of Faith," and the *Epistles* of Horace, which many adolescents first read in school. Moraley's familiarity with the Bible is apparent in his quotations from and references to the psalms and the New Testament. In addition to these books, Moraley read plays, novels, and poetry. Several public libraries provided Londoners with relatively easy access to books. And in the used-book market in Moorfields, "saunt'ring 'prentices" gathered at the stalls to read Restoration dramatists (Thomas Otway and William Congreve were favorites), while "Pleased semp-stresses" became engrossed in Alexander Pope's "Rape of the Lock."[1] Moraley twice included in his memoirs his own attempts at poetry, although both pieces built on the work of others. His prose is at times self-consciously poetic, as in "Then the green Fields and verdant Meadows display their several Beauties, advantageous to the joyful Shepherd" (107), although his writing generally resembles the more

1. John Gay, "Trivia; or, The Art of Walking the Streets of London" (1716), in *Poems of John Gay*, ed. John Underhill, 2 vols. (London: Routledge, 1893), 1:147–48.

straightforward style of Daniel Defoe. The title of Moraley's memoirs makes obvious reference to the literature of "unfortunates." These popular novels and autobiographies—*The Unfortunate General* (1713), *Unfortunate Heiress* (1726), *Unfortunate Dutchess* (1739), *Unfortunate Englishman* (1742), *Unfortunate Concubines* (1748), *Unfortunate Mother* (1761), and even another voyager to New Jersey and Pennsylvania, *The Unfortunate Husbandman* (1784)—focused on the lives and opinions of common men and women and reflected the new and expanding eighteenth-century reading public.

While in the colonies Moraley also read almanacs. George Webb's poem about Philadelphia, which appeared in Titan Leeds's *Almanac* for 1730, is reproduced below as an example of the type of poetry Moraley thought he could improve.[2] Moraley shortened, rearranged, and added a few lines to the original.

Goddess of Numbers, who art wont to rove
O'er the gay Landskip, or the smiling Grove;
Who taught me first to sing in humble Strains,
Of murm'ring Fountains, and of flowery Plains,
Assist me now; while I in Verse repeat
The heavenly Beauties of thy Fav'rite Seat.

Teach me, O Goddess, in harmonious Lays,
To sing thy much-lov'd *Pennsylvania's* Praise;
Thy *Philadelphia's* Beauties to indite,
In Verse as tuneful as her Sons can write:
Such as from B——l's Pen are wont to flow,
Or more judicious T——r's us'd to show.

Stretch'd on the Bank of *Delaware's* rapid Stream
Stands *Philadelphia*, not unkown to Fame:
Here the tall Vessels safe at Anchor ride,
And *Europe's* Wealth flows in with every Tide:
Thro' each wide Ope the distant Prospect's clear;
The well-built Streets are regularly fair:

The Plan by thee contriv'd, O *Penn*, the Scheme,
A Work immortal as the Founder's Name.
'Tis here *Apollo* does erect his Throne,
This his *Parnassus*, this his *Helicon*:
Here solid Sense does every Bosom warm,
Here Noise and Nonsense have forgot to charm.

2. George Webb, in Titan Leeds, *The Genuine Leeds Almanac for . . . 1730* (Philadelphia: Leeds, 1730).

Thy Seers how cautious! and how gravely wise!
Thy hopeful Youth in Emulation rise:
Who (if the wishing Muse inspir'd does sing)
Shall Liberal Arts to such Perfection bring,
Europe shall mourn her ancient Fame declin'd,
And *Philadelphia* be the *Athens* of Mankind.

Thy lovely Daughters unaffected shine,
In each Perfection, every Grace divine:
Beauty triumphant sits in every Eye,
And Wit shines forth, but check'd with Modesty;
Decently Grave, which shows a sober Sense,
And Chearful too, a Sign of Innocence.

But what. O *Pennsylvania* does declare
Thy Bliss, speaks thee profusely happy: here
Sweet *Liberty* her gentle Influence sheds,
And *Peace* her downy Wings about us spreads:
While War and Desolation widely reigns,
And Captive Nations groan beneath their Chains.

While half the World implicitly obey,
Some lawless Tyrant's most imperious Sway
No threatning Trumpet warns us from afar
Of hastning Miseries or approaching War;
Fearless the Hind pursues his wonted Toil,
And eats the Product of his grateful Soil.

No unjust Sentence we have Cause to fear
No arbitrary Monarch rules us here.
Our Lives, our Properties, and all that's ours,
Our happy Constitution here secures.
What Praise and Thanks, O *Penn*! are due to thee!
For this first perfect Scheme of Liberty!

How shall the Muse thy just Applauses sing?
Or in what Strains due Acclamations bring?
Who can thy Charter read, but with Surprize
Must strait proclaim thee Generous, Just and Wise?
Thro' every Page, thro' every careful Line,
Now does the Friend, the Nursing Father shine!

What Toils, what Perils didst thou under go,
Thro' scorching Heats, thro' endless Tracts of Snow?
How scorning Ease didst tempt the raging Floods?

How hew thy Passage thro' untrodden Woods?
Thine was the Danger, Thine was all the Toil;
While We, ungrateful We, divide the Spoil.

O cou'd my Verse a Monument but raise,
Some Part, some little Sketch of thy due Praise,
When Time, the Tomb, or Statue shall destroy,
Or *Philadelphia's* Self in Dust shall lye,
Ages to come should read thy Favourite Name,
Fresh and immortal in the Book of Fame.

APPENDIX E: NEWCASTLE, ENGLAND

In 1723 the Moraley family moved from London, a metropolis of perhaps 750,000 people, to northeastern England's Newcastle-upon-Tyne, a substantially smaller town that contained approximately 18,000 inhabitants and was the ancestral home of the Moraleys.[1] Despite its smaller size, Newcastle, according to one visitor, "most resembles London of any place in England," in part because the "shops are good and of Distinct trades, not selling many things in one shop as is ye Custom in most Country towns and Cittys."[2] Family connections, a specialized retail economy, and a busy port made Newcastle a likely place to recoup the family's fortunes. Daniel Defoe vividly describes the town during the 1720s:

> From [Durham] the road to Newcastle gives a view of the inexhausted store of coals and coal pits, from whence not London only, but all the south part of England is continually supplied. . . . Newcastle is a spacious, extended, infinitely populous place; 'tis seated upon the River Tyne, which is here a noble, large and deep river, and ships of any reasonable burthen may come

1. P. M. Horsley, *Eighteenth-Century Newcastle* (Newcastle: Oriel, 1971), 220.
2. Celia Fiennes, *Through England on a Side Saddle* (London: Field & Tuer, 1888), 176–77.

safely up to the very town. . . . The situation of the town to the landward is exceeding unpleasant, and the buildings very close and old, standing on the declivity of two exceeding high hills, which, together with the smoke of the coals, makes it not the pleasantest place in the world to live in; but it is made amends abundantly by the goodness of the river, which runs between the two hills, and which, as I said, bringing ships up to the very quays, and fetching the coals down from the country, makes it a place of very great business. . . . They build ships here to perfection, I mean as to strength, and firmness, and to bear the sea; and as the coal trade occasions a demand for such strong ships, a great many are built here. This gives an addition to the merchants' business, in requiring a supply of all sorts of naval stores to fit out those ships. Here is also a considerable manufacture of hard ware, or wrought iron, lately erected after the manner of Sheffield, which is very helpful for employing the poor, of which this town has always a prodigious number.[3]

3. Daniel Defoe, *A Tour Through the Whole Island of Great Britain*, ed. Pat Rogers (Aylesbury, Eng.: Penguin, 1971), 535–37.

APPENDIX F: ISAAC PEARSON'S SERVANTS

Isaac Pearson, Moraley's master, advertised for three runaway servants in the newspapers between 1727 and 1737. The advertisement for the first escapee appeared in the March 30—April 6, 1727, edition of the *American Weekly Mercury*:

> Run away on the 3rd of this Instant April, from Isaac Pearson of Burlington, a Servant Man, he is a short well set Fellow, and Purblind, named ——— ——— about 30 Years of Age, round Visage, his Hair cut off; he has on an old Hat, a redish strip'd Cap, a dark Drugget Pea Jacket, and a striped Flannel Jacket with blue stripes under the same, a pair of Ozenbrig Drawers, and round Toed Shoes. Whoever secures the said Servant so that his Master may have him again, shall have 40 Shillings Reward and reasonable Charges.

Figure 17 reproduces the notice for Aaron Middleton, and Pearson advertised for a third servant in the August 25—September 1, 1737, issue of the *Pennsylvania Gazette*:

> Run away from Isaac Pearson, of Burlington, in West-New-Jersey, a Servant Man named John Williams, aged about 37 Years, a West-Country

Man, speaks by Clusters, hard to understand, very short, square set, by Trade a Clockmaker: He had on a full-trimm'd brown colour'd cloth Coat, with flat Pearl Buttons set in Brass, a flannel strip'd Jacket with blue Flaps, a fine Shirt, and an Ozenbrigs one, ozenbrigs Trousers, blue worsted Stockings, peaked toe'd Shoes, with Hobnails drove in the Heels, a narrow brim'd castor Hat.

Whoever secures the said Servant so that he may be had again, shall have Thirty Shillings Reward, paid by Isaac Pearson.

APPENDIX G: THE GHOST IN ISAAC PEARSON'S HOME

In 1686 a notorious case had occurred in what would be Moraley's residence in Burlington. James Wills was indicted for murdering his African bondswoman. One witness at the trial heard noises "and supposed it to be James Wills beating his Negro woman, and heard many Lashes more and Crying out, untill hee was greevd and went into his owne house and shut the dore, and said to his wife oh! yond cruell man, and sayth hee beleeves hee heard full a hundred stripes or lashes." Despite similar testimony from other witnesses, Wills was acquitted on the grounds that the unnamed woman died from long-standing health problems rather than from the beating.[1] Isaac Pearson purchased the Wills estate on the west side of High Street in 1715.[2]

Many if not most seventeenth- and eighteenth-century Europeans and Americans believed in ghosts. One element of most ghost stories was that the apparition

1. H. Clay Reed and George J. Miller, *The Burlington Court Book: A Record of Quaker Jurisprudence in West New Jersey, 1680–1709* (Washington, D.C.: American Historical Association, 1944), 56–57. For a further discussion of this case, see Ernest Lyght, *Path of Freedom: The Black Presence in New Jersey's Burlington County, 1659–1900* (Cherry Hill, N.J.: E & E Publishing, 1978).

2. Robert Thompson, City of Burlington Historic Commission (Typed memo, March 4, 1986, in "Pearson-How House File," Burlington County Historical Society).

always had a specific reason for appearing. A popular superstition in and around Newcastle, England, held that "though justice should fail in detecting the murderer, yet went he not without punishment even on earth, for not unfrequently did the spirit of his victim appear to him in the darkness and solitude of night, filling his mind with terror, to which death would have been to him a relief, had he not dreaded the greater torments which awaited him hereafter."[3]

3. On the belief in ghosts in early modern England and America, see Keith Thomas, *Religion and the Decline of Magic* (New York: Charles Scribner's Sons, 1971), 587–99. Quotation from Richardson, *The Local Historian's Table Book*, 1 (pt. 2): 34.

APPENDIX H: THE WITCHCRAFT TRIAL AT MOUNT HOLLY

Only two accounts of the witchcraft "trial" at Mount Holly, New Jersey, survive. The article published in the *Pennsylvania Gazette* by Benjamin Franklin, which he may or may not have authored, is considered a "hoax" by the editors of Franklin's papers.[1] But Moraley offers a second report, which seemingly confirms many of its details. The stories share a number of similarities: two people were accused; the tests consisted of both weighing the suspects against the Bible and floating them on water; and the two ordeals failed to prove demonic possession. At one point the language of the two versions is virtually identical. Moraley observed that "to the Surprise of the Beholders, [the suspects] weighed down both Prophets and Apostles" (124), while Franklin's article stated that "to the great Surprize of the Spectators, . . . [the accused] were too heavy for *Moses* and all the Prophets and Apostles." Moreover, both reporters were extremely skeptical of the proceedings.

Yet the two accounts contain several discrepancies. Moraley dated the trial as taking place in September 1734, four years after the newspaper story. He simply may have forgotten to describe the episode in the proper sequence while writing

1. Leonard W. Labaree and Whitfield J. Bell Jr., eds., *The Papers of Benjamin Franklin* (New Haven: Yale University Press, 1959–), 1:182.

his memoirs and, rather than rewrite the draft, decided to sidetrack himself in his narrative in order to recount the event. Moraley identified the suspects as two elderly women whose facial features had made them suspicious, while the *Gazette* specified that the accused were a man and a woman who had enchanted local barnyard animals.

It is doubtful that Moraley merely retold the story based on his hazy recollection of Franklin's newspaper article, because Moraley, unlike the newspaper, identified Jonathan Wright as the local justice who presided over the trial. And Wright, an influential and wealthy Quaker, was a good candidate for the role. In 1713 he moved from Chesterfield to Burlington, where he resided until his death in 1742, at which time he owned 1,600 acres of land, several improved lots, and a tanyard. Wright served repeatedly as the local representative to the quarterly meeting of the Quakers and participated actively in town politics and in judicial affairs on the county level. Moreover, Wright did fit the description in the newspaper article. He had a wife, Elizabeth Fretwell, in 1730; he was a county constable beginning in 1719; and he was commissioned Justice of the Peace in 1732 and may well have served in that capacity previously. According to his will, Wright also owned "a large quarto Bible,"[2] perhaps not unlike the one used in the trial. Whether Wright was also a "grave tall Man," as Franklin's story specified, is unknown.

Wright may have been induced to stage this mock trial, not to prosecute witches but to acquit the innocent victims of popular prejudice in response to the following petition, which was in circulation among Burlington Quakers prior to 1730:

> Please your Worships, gentlemen. Pray doe have some Charety for me, a poor Distrest man that is become old and scars able to Mentain my Famely at the best, and now sum Peopel has raised a Reporte that my Wife is a Witch, by which I and my famely must sartinly suffer if she cant be clear'd of the thing and a Stop Poot to the Reporte for Peopel will not have no Delings with me on the acount[.] Pray Gentlemen I beg the favor of you that one or more of you would free her for she is Desirous that she may be tried by all Maner of Ways that ever a Woman was tried so that she can get

2. William Wade Hinshaw, *Encyclopedia of American Quaker Genealogy*, 9 vols. (Richmond, Ind.: Edwards, 1938), 2:249; Henry H. Bisbee and Rebecca Bisbee Colesar, eds., *The Burlington Town Book, 1694–1785* (Burlington, N.J.: Bisbee, 1975); Wills, 2:550; Larry C. Wright, *Wright's 400 Years-Plus: Thirteen Generation Family* (Amarillo, Tex.: Wright, 1984), 12–18; George Gates Radden Jr., comp., "The Wrights of West New Jersey," 3 vols. (Manuscript in the James Duncan Philips Library of the Essex Institute Library, Salem, Mass., 1953–63), 1:19; Minutes of the Burlington Monthly Meeting, Burlington County Historical Society.

Wright fell from grace in 1739 when he was disowned by the meeting for reasons that had nothing to do with witchcraft, and his attempts to gain reinstatement failed.

> Cleare of the Report[.] from your poor and Humble Servant, Jeames Moore.[3]

This petition supports the newspaper's contention that the accused voluntarily appeared and were desirous of a trial, as well as Moraley's claim that it was the facial features of old women that brought them the reputation of witchery.

Indeed, it is possible that Moraley, who was living in Mount Holly in 1730, acted as the source for the newspaper article. This could account for the article's two London references: "after the Manner of *Moorfields*" and "as solemnly as the Sword-bearer of *London* before the Lord Mayor."[4] Another explanation is that the newspaper account helped shape contemporary gossip about the event. The newspaper piece from the October 15–22, 1730, issue of the *Pennsylvania Gazette* follows.

> BURLINGTON, Oct. 12. Saturday last at *Mount-Holly*, about 8 Miles from this Place, near 300 People were gathered together to see an Experiment or two tried on some Persons accused of Witchcraft. It seems the Accused had been charged with making their Neighbours Sheep dance in an uncommon Manner, and with causing Hogs to speak, and sing Psalms, &c. to the great Terror and Amazement of the King's good and peaceable Subjects in this Province; and the Accusers being very positive that if the Accused were weighed in Scales against a Bible, the Bible would prove too heavy for them;[5] or that, if they were bound and put into the River, they would swim;[6] the said Accused desirous to make their Innocence appear, voluntarily offered to undergo the said Trials, if 2 of the most violent of their Accusers would be tried with them. Accordingly the Time and Place was agreed on, and advertised about the Country; The Accusers were 1

3. Quoted in Amelia Mott Gummere, *Witchcraft and Quakerism: A Study in Social History* (Philadelphia: Biddle, 1908), 56.

4. A popular gathering place, "Moorfields" was an area near the outskirts of London just north of the guild hall, royal exchange, and other locales associated with Moraley and his family. The solemnity of the "Sword-bearer of *London* before the Lord Mayor" refers to the manner in which he proceeded, described as follows: "When the Mayor goes out of the precincts of the City a sceptre, a sword, and a cap are borne before him, and he is followed by the principal Aldermen in scarlet gowns with gold chains, himself and they on horseback" (Walter Besant, *London in the Time of the Stuarts* [London: Black, 1903], 334).

5. Because witches assumed spectral shapes, the Bible, as a literally and figuratively substantial book of God, would outweigh insubstantial witches. See Marion L. Starkey, *The Devil in Massachusetts* (New York: Time Inc., 1949), 37ff.

6. The following observation about witches by James I was a popular belief: "God hath appoynted (for a super-naturell signe of the monstrous impietie of Witches) that the water shall refuse to receive them in her bosom, that have shaken off them the sacred water of Baptisme" (as quoted in R. Trevor Davies, *Four Centuries of Witch Beliefs* [London: Methuen, 1947], 47).

Man and 1 Woman; and the Accused the same. The Parties being met, and the People got together, a grand Consultation was held, before they proceeded to Trial; in which it was agreed to use the Scales first; and a Committee of Men were appointed to search the Men, and a Committee of Women to search the Women, to see if they had any Thing of Weight about them, particularly Pins.[7] After the Scrutiny was over, a huge great Bible belonging to the Justice of the Place was provided, and a Lane through the Populace was made from the Justices House to the Scales, which were fixed on a Gallows erected for that Purpose opposite to the House, that the Justice's Wife and the rest of the Ladies might see the Trial, without coming amongst the Mob; and after the Manner of *Moorfields*, a large Ring was also made. Then came out of the House a grave tall Man carrying the Holy Writ before the supposed Wizard, &c. (as solemnly as the Sword-bearer of *London* before the Lord Mayor) the Wizard was first put in the Scale, and over him was read a Chapter out of the Books of *Moses*,[8] and then the Bible was put in the other Scale, (which being kept down before) was immediately let go; but to the great Surprize of the Spectators, Flesh and Bones came down plump, and outweighed that great good Book by abundance. After the same Manner, the others were served, and their Lumps of Mortality severally were too heavy for *Moses* and all the Prophets and Apostles. This being over, the Accusers and the rest of the Mob, not satisfied with this Experiment, would have the Trial by Water; accordingly a most solemn Procession was made to the Mill-pond; where both Accused and Accusers being stripp'd (saving only to the Women their Shifts) were bound Hand and Foot, and severally placed in the Water, lengthways, from the Side of a Barge or Flat, having for Security only a Rope about the Middle of each, which was held by some in the Flat. The Accuser Man being thin and spare, with some Difficulty began to sink at last; but the rest every one of them swam very light upon the Water. A Sailor in the Flat jump'd out upon the Back of the Man accused, thinking to drive him down to the Bottom; but the Person bound, without any Help, came up some time before the other. The Woman Accuser, being told that she did not sink, would be duck'd a second Time; when she swam again as light as before. Upon which she declared, That she believed the

7. Witches commonly used domestic items like pins as weapons; see Carol F. Karlsen, *The Devil in the Shape of a Woman: Witchcraft in Colonial New England* (New York: Vintage, 1987), 6–14.

8. See the Fifth Book of Moses, Deuteronomy 18:10–12: "There shall not be found among you *any one* that maketh his son or his daughter to pass through the fire, or that useth divination, or an observer of times, or an enchanter, or a witch, or a charmer, or a consulter with familiar spirits, or a wizard, or a necromancer. For all that do these things are an abomination unto the Lord: and because of these abominations the Lord thy God doth drive them out from before thee."

Accused had bewitched her to make her so light, and that she would be duck'd again a Hundred Times, but she would duck the Devil out of her. The accused Man, being surpriz'd at his own Swimming, was not so confident of his Innocence as before, but said, *If I am a Witch, it is more than I know*. The more thinking Part of the Spectators were of Opinion, that any Person so bound and plac'd in the Water (unless they were mere Skin and Bones) would swim till their Breath was gone, and their lungs fill'd with Water. But it being the general Belief of the populace, that the Womens Shifts, and the Garters with which they were bound help'd to support them; it is said they are to be tried again the next warm Weather, naked.

INDEX